INSIDE THE KU KLUX KLAN:

The Rise and Fall of a Grand Dragon

Brian Tackett

authorHOUSE®

AuthorHouse™
1663 Liberty Drive
Bloomington, IN 47403
www.authorhouse.com
Phone: 1-800-839-8640

First published by AuthorHouse 9/11/2009

ISBN: 978-1-4490-2897-8 (e)
ISBN: 978-1-4389-7311-1 (sc)
ISBN: 978-1-4490-2896-1 (hc)

Library of Congress Control Number: 2009903038

Printed in the United States of America
Bloomington, Indiana

This book is printed on acid-free paper.

Dedication:

To the many people who have been and remain dear to me I hope this will explain some of the blanks in my life.

TABLE OF CONTENTS

PART IV – APEX OF POWER

PART V - BETRAYAL

To The Reader:

What you are about to read is a true account of my days as a Grand Dragon in the Ku Klux Klan. I have used only first names to protect the innocent, and where necessary, I have changed the names entirely.

Brian G. Tackett

PROLOGUE

When a man thinks he is presently going to die, his behavior changes markedly. I suppose some men face that prospect with the courage of one who knows he has served God well and will be rewarded in the afterlife. The man kneeling in front of me did not seem to have that confidence.

His name was Jared, but everyone called him Timbo. At five feet eight inches tall, one hundred and sixty pounds or so, he was not much more than one of those homeless people you might see living in a box on the corner alley of any major city.

His long, stringy brown hair was dirty, likely unwashed for days. His beard, if you could call it that, looked more like a drought stricken weed garden than a finely groomed lawn. On his knees, with his hands tied behind his back, he was leaning forward alternately begging me, then not, to kill him. Oddly, when he pleaded to God for salvation, he didn't look up at all, only down.

"Please don't do this to me, mister," he sobbed. "Please God, don't let this happen." His voice was grief stricken, a quiet tone one uses when he knows he is helpless to change anything. He didn't know, at that point, what he was here for. Before waking up in this predicament his last conscious thought was probably of the heavy-chested hooker who was on her way back to the bed from the motel room bathroom. She had slipped the tranquilizer in his drink several minutes before, and called to let me know when to come get him. She said he was asleep, and that's exactly how we found him.

I was standing in front of him now, fully robed, with two of my brothers, one on each side of him to keep him from getting up, although he didn't seem interested in trying to resist.

The four of us were all alone on a muddy riverbank that gently sloped down to a swift torrent. It was at the edge of a section of bottomland common to the rivers in the Tennessee River Valley area. Not even the farmer who owned this parcel knew we were there, and he never would. I didn't know who owned it. For several years I had been coming here to hunt, fish and otherwise simply find my bearings in life when the world seemed a bit too crowded. Since I had spent a lot of time here, I was sure that no one else would be around at 2:00 a.m. in the morning.

I eased my buck knife from its sheath in front of Timbo. He began to scream, and the echoes from the woods amplified the eeriness of the night.

"Go ahead and blindfold him," I instructed my brothers. I wanted him to see the large blade before I blindfolded him. One of my hooded associates removed a long piece of a green army blanket we had cut for the occasion, and tied it around Timbo's head to cover his eyes. Timbo started to tremble.

I removed my robe and hood, walked up to the truck and put them inside. I wouldn't need them anymore. I removed a pair of thick rubber gloves that extended to the elbow and returned to the riverbank.

The river was swollen, and the truck headlights made an ominous glow on the water. I walked to the water's edge, took my lock blade pocket knife from my pants, and bent over to rinse it, not that it was dirty. I was stalling for time to build up my nerve for what I knew I had to do. Meanwhile, my brothers had removed their robes and hoods as well and placed them in the van parked just on the other side of my truck – the van in which Timbo had arrived to this horrible moment.

I stood, wiped the blade on my jeans, and walked back up to where Timbo still knelt in the mud. I remembered the old man's voice, the man who sent me here to do this, who simply gave the orders and who must have known what I was going through right this minute. He must have known that this would make or break me. That's why his henchmen were here I supposed, to carry it out if I refused.

I didn't know these partners in crime, my "brothers." We had met briefly at the old man's house when the plan was made. They were out-of-towners for sure, but from where, I didn't have a clue.

"He raped the girl!" I could hear the old man saying that night. "I know she has been a little wild, but at fifteen years old, she can't be expected to know any better. That son-of-a-bitch took advantage of her, damn-it, and when she refused, he raped her!"

"But, I thought they were, like, dating or whatever?" I had asked lamely.

"Dating my ass! He was stringing her out on drugs just to use her. He's done this shit before, but now he's done it to the wrong one. I want you to handle it."

All his life, Timbo had been in trouble. Sometimes it was trouble with the law, sometimes it was trouble with guys like me. No one liked him. He was the guy always standing on the street corner trying to look cool, but instead looking like a junkie after a fix. If you talked to him, you immediately realized that he was a con man, and a poor one at that. Nevertheless, people who didn't know him would occasionally fall for his lines of bull. Of course, afterward, when they realized he had stolen their money or otherwise failed to live up to his promised, they would want to kill him. But that didn't bother Timbo. He kept right on selling the bullshit, in five gallon buckets, to anyone who would buy.

Mostly, he wanted money for drugs. He would say he had a good source for this drug or that drug; today heroin, tomorrow marijuana, and the next day it might be methamphetamine. Inevitably, someone would give him the money to go get it, since he would say that he alone could go because the dealer wouldn't sell it to him if anyone else was around.

He might or might not come back, depending on if he thought he might see you again. If he did return, there would be a story about how the guy didn't have that deal anymore, but Timbo had found something else, just as good, at a little higher price. Or he may return with just what you ordered, though it would be cut, if it were cuttable, so that he could skim a good portion for himself. He was a little weasel of a man, and it wouldn't hurt society one bit to bury him and get it over with.

"I guess you're right," I heard myself answering the old man, not sure whether he was or not. I had heard Timbo had a problem with the girl. She was what I called a tease, and a young one. I always assumed that she was promiscuous, and that was in fact her reputation. It was the fact that she was the daughter of one of the old man's friends that made her important. I could have told the old man that she might have been lying about Timbo, but I didn't. I could have made a case on Timbo's behalf; argued that the girl knew everyone would believe her because no one liked him. But I didn't. I could have pointed out that the girl was mad at Timbo because she caught him with another girl, and had every reason to lie. For whatever reason that men do not argue with the boss, I didn't.

I reflected on this as I looked down at poor, helpless Timbo. He couldn't have been over twenty years old, yet he looked almost forty. Drug abuse, they say, causes a person to age fast, and here was the proof. What I was about to do would age him even more, perhaps eventually kill him, even though not as a direct result of tonight. It would be the lingering effects that would devastate and demoralize him, depriving him of the will to live. Someone, sometime in the future, would be seeing Timbo as I see him now, humbled, near death, helpless.

"Timbo," I said. "Do you know why you're here? You're here because you raped a little girl, and she didn't like that. You're here to pay for that Timbo, and I am here to collect."

"I swear to God I didn't do it!" he screamed at me. He began to tremble, almost like he was going into shock. When you hear the truth, you know it, and I believed Timbo had just told me the absolute truth. Or maybe I just wanted to believe him because rape allegations had become so common and were made with little evidence. I was always suspect of any such claim by a disgruntled female, especially a young, vengeful one. I couldn't exonerate this man, unfortunately, no matter how wrong I thought the accusation was.

To my two associates, I said. "Get his pants down." On the farm, as a boy growing up, a sharp lock-blade pocket knife was all I needed to castrate and de-tail the small pigs. I couldn't see the need for anything more tonight. My brothers wrestled Timbo out of his pants, spread him out on the muddy bank, and I performed the operation as quickly as possible. Timbo damn near deafened me with screams that would make any two-year old envious. I remember thinking that we should have gagged him. After the operation, I slapped some black mud from the riverbank between his legs to slow the bleeding. I stood up and turned toward the water, and threw what was in my hand out as far as possible. I looked for a long while after the splash.

Vaguely, between Timbo's sobs, I heard one of my brother Klansman say: "Congratulations, you just made *Grand Dragon*."

CHAPTER ONE
Rumors and Myths: The Fear and Lure of The White Knights

In south-central Kentucky where I was raised until my early teens, the rumors of the Ku Klux Klan run rampant. They are believed to be all around you, yet unidentifiable, even aloof from the every day activities of local inhabitants. They are almost like spirits that hover, invisibly, to see every move you make. It is not something a man thinks about all the time, but occasionally, when the subject comes up in casual conversation, the feeling that they are out there, somewhere, collecting together secretly to impose punishment for transgressions, comes over you like a wet blanket.

Who they are, and where they might be, is beyond the common resident. Unless you are a part of them, you simply do not know who they are, where they live, or what they intend to do at any given time. They have always been known to appear out of nowhere, mass together to inflict some social disorder, and then disappear as quickly as they came. To the outside observer, they seem to have a collective magical power.

I first heard the myths surrounding the Klan as a child on my parent's farm in Bowling Green, Kentucky. My father had bought the place in 1974, and went into business as a small part time farmer. Because there was so much work to be done, he hired numerous seasonal workers to put up fences, level ground, and harvest the various crops that we grew each year. It was from these locals, mostly ex-convicts that I acquired much of my working knowledge about my community, particularly the Klan.

Charles, a thirty year old worker and his brother were there one hot summer day relaxing after our noon lunch break. We were sitting under two large cedar trees just off the back part of the main house. They had been employees of my father for as long as I could remember, and were a couple of my favorites. I didn't mind at all that they were a little slow. It was that disability which prevented them from holding a decent paying job for any length of time, making farm work their most stable profession.

We had finished eating our bologna sandwiches, washing them down with lemonade when Charlie and his brother began talking about the Klan. How the subject was brought up, I can't recall. I think it must have been some event involving the KKK, perhaps, with hindsight, a march or rally. Instantly my ears perked up, this was something that always had my attention even at seven years of age. I paid close attention to everything any adult said around me. In fact, at that age, a seven year old couldn't wait to grow up and become an adult who had all this vast knowledge they shared so freely around me.

"Remember when they hung them three niggers *down't* Russellville," Charlie said to his brother. "They *wuz messin'* with them white girls, an' didn't stop when they was told to." "Hung *'em* in the yard, didn't they?" his brother said. "Yep, All three of *'em*. *Musta* been, around sixty-three or so", Charlie replied. "That's what I'm *a-thinkin'*. *Ain't* been no niggers fooling' with any white girls down there since, I *knowed* of," said his brother.

"There *wuz* a bunch of *'em* round here too. *Cept ain't* nobody knows who they is. Some of *'em* is lawyers, doctors, even judges. I *reckin'* all the damn law is Klan," Charlie continued.

I knew where Russellville was. My dad had driven me all over the area. He was in construction and would take me with him on some of his excavation job sites. Whenever I rode with him to Russellville I would ask him how long it was going to take to get there, and he would answer me in minutes, so I figured it was probably about thirty minutes away from our farm.

I had never given any thought to interracial relations, or the Klan, and I had never considered that the important people in our town were members. Like others, I had seen the movies which showed the Klan burning houses and lighting crosses. At seven years old, I had believed the Klan lived in the deep South which to me was on the other side of the world, not in the same place I lived. Charlie and his brother said they lived here, right here, and that left me with an uneasy feeling, a prelude to my future.

Years went by and we all grew up. Through these years I would often hear more and more about the Klan. It was just a little here and a little there, like, "hey did you know that his dad is in the KKK", or "I saw him going down that road where the KKK go", but you didn't really know if the rumors were true or not. It was those type of rumors, together with sketchy history taught in school that gave me the mythical impression of the KKK.

Looking back, I believe the impression I had was the result of what I believed to be "white guilt." All the history classes I had taken in school mysteriously omitted discussions of the KKK, treating it like a blemish on our past which should be forgotten, not studied. From this result, my education about this group came solely from rumors and backyard stories. I never found the truth about the KKK and was forced to accept the stories. I know now that even the black children knew about as much as I did about them and our lessons were taught to us in the wrong way.

Teaching of the KKK was an error in the school curriculum and hopefully my writing of this book will be a helpful cure. To allow our young to be drawn to a mystery, or in the case of black children, to be taught to hate all whites as probable Klan is disastrous. This farce is only because we are too ashamed of our past to talk about it, and it makes our lives a travesty. There is no doubt in my mind that the collective guilt of the white society in which I was raised kept the Klan a hidden, dark secret. I believe this contributed greatly to the lure of the KKK. Had I been taught the truth about the KKK in school, I might not be telling this story now.

Generally speaking, not many people are members of the KKK. Not in my community and not in this country. While there are some political and civil servant members, their numbers are not as great as the rumors would have one to believe. Do they wield power? Are they a force to beware of? Not as a group of members of the Klan are they a force, but only as a set of beliefs among the uneducated, poor, country whites and blacks are they powerful. These beliefs about the meaning of history and the meaning of racial differences are a serious force in our society that have produced, beyond any reasonable doubt, some of the grossest tragedies in our recent history. It is time we made a concerted effort to deal with this problem in a structured, well reasoned manner. Before any of us can do that, we must be truthful; first to ourselves and then to the world at large.

If we have been programmed to hate by sketchy history and rumor, we need to admit that. If we have learned to hate because of the way we have been treated, or because of what we have been told, we need to admit that as well; as politically incorrect as it seems. Until we learn to admit the truth, we can go no further down the road of knowledge.

My story really begins with the Imperial Wizard of the local chapter of the KKK, called the "Kentucky Knights of the Ku Klux Klan." I had the misfortune of being introduced to that organization directly by *him*. In other words, I was brought in at the top. Maybe that is what makes my story so odd.

CHAPTER TWO
Meeting The Wizard

Bowling Green, Kentucky sits about twenty miles north of the Tennessee-Kentucky state line, half-way across the state. It is not far from the birth place of Jefferson Davis, the father of the Confederacy. In 1990, the population was 41,688 with the major industry being farming, mostly cattle farming. There are several factories including the famous General Motors Corvette Plant which employ several thousand. Bowling Green is the largest city within a sixty-mile radius.

The city itself is an example of urban sprawl. There are no high rises, (city hall, the jail and the federal courthouse all share the same downtown block). The growth has always been in the suburbs.

To the Northeast and west runs the Barren River. Only two bridges cross it, forcing most of the expansion in the other three directions. Within a few miles to the west, a ridge of hills begin and rise up to a thousand feet or so. Towards the east the land is rolling and has supported the brunt of the expanding population and the commercial growth.

My family moved to Bowling Green in 1970. After working a few years in the service station business, my dad bought a backhoe and went into excavating. By the time I was in the second grade, I was riding along on the equipment with him, learning how to do all types of excavation and to operate backhoes, bull dozers and to drive dump trucks.

By the time I was seventeen, I began working as a foreman for Valley Construction, a one-horse construction company owned by a local doctor. We had a dump truck, backhoe, small dozer, and a trailer. We advertised in the newspaper to do custom excavating, including land clearing, septic tank installation and anything else that required digging or grading. I had a pager and the doctor supplied a blue Ford Ranger four-wheel drive pickup for my transportation. It was a fantastic opportunity for me at that age. I was more a partner than a foreman, and possessed complete discretion in obtaining jobs and pricing them; as well as the unfettered power to hire and fire employees. I would respond to customer calls, bid jobs, move equipment, hire and supervise employees to perform the work to the customer's satisfaction and then collect the money – all with no oversight whatsoever. I didn't have a salary as such, just a share of the net proceeds – whatever share I thought I deserved. It was a job which would bring me face-to-face with the Ku Klux Klan.

On a warm Spring day in 1988, I received a call to meet a man at a small townhouse in the city to haul off some old roofing. When I arrived, an old man was standing out front next to a black, four-wheel drive Chevrolet pickup truck. He was short and thin with a weathered face and a dark tan. He was wearing work boots, jeans, a ball cap with a frayed bill, and a dark t-shirt, one small pocket on the upper left side full of folded papers as well as an ink pen or two. He looked like any other carpenter I had been in contact with. In front of the garage, I could see a car sized pile of old roofing.

"Afternoon sir," I said as I exited my truck. "I'm the man you spoke to on the phone." The old man eyed me keenly. "Reckon' you can haul this stuff off for me?" he asked without further introduction. I walked over to the pile and took a closer look. It was filled with nails. I would have to be careful because any nail in a tire would cost me any profit I could hope to make on the job. "When you want it done?"

"How much you charge?" And that's the way it always went. Everyone wanted to know how much before anything else. I don't know how people do business in other places, but in Kentucky, the bottom line comes first, followed by the bullshit.

"I'll need a three-hour minimum for the truck and backhoe, but the job will be done in an hour or so. I'll do it for one hundred and fifty dollars, that's a sixty dollar break," I answered. What the hell, I needed the work and it was an easy job. He said yes, and we agreed that I would do it the next day while he was still putting on the new roof.

The next afternoon, I finished the job and waited to see the old man for my money. He walked up to me and asked if a check was okay with me. "I'd rather have cash, but if that's all you got," I replied. Sometimes personal checks bounced and I didn't want the hassle of having to collect.

"Can you come up to my house later? I can run over to the bank and get cash and meet you back there", he offered. That was fine with me. If I had taken the check and cashed it myself, who knows? I might not have seen that old man again.

It was after dark when I arrived at the old man's house after dropping off my equipment and taking my employee home. As I pulled in, my headlights shown over old cars, tractors, trucks, and miscellaneous farm equipment parked in a grassy field on the left side of the drive. To my right, I could make out a large yard with a couple of oak trees. The most conspicuous thing about the place was a large pond which lay between the house and the road. His place lay atop a hill from which the city of Bowling Green was clearly visible and I could see the city lights as I turned and idled toward the house. A dog which could have passed for a small brown bear appeared. I hadn't seen him and now he was trying to take off my front tire. I turned off my engine and lights while the dog patiently waited by my door, salivating. I honked my horn.

The old man came out, called something to the dog which prompted it to disappear behind the house, and began to walk out. I rolled down my window and the smell of frying food filled the air. "Come on in. The old lady has dinner ready," he said as he approached my door.

We walked probably a hundred yards from where I was parked and stepped up on the front porch. We entered through a wooden front door and looking down, I could see that the flooring was wood also. To my left sat an old wood stove and on my right, I could see a couch and chair arranged in an "L" shape along the wall. Standing as if the room had been built around it, was a podium. I had seen them in school, but seeing one in a house was a different story. Still observing my surroundings, I noticed that next to the podium, hidden partially by a chair, was a large square wooden table. Glancing around the room again, I realized that I was standing in a ready made meeting hall. Through an opening to my left, directly across from the stove, I could see a kitchen and in it was another square wooden table. It was covered with a white tablecloth and several bowls of food.

Walking towards the kitchen with the aroma of food filling my nostrils, I realized that there was a lot of food for just a few people. In fact, the food could have fed about ten or more. "Hope you found the place all right", the old man said as we were going through the door. I didn't expect to eat here, so I tried to turn down the silent offer. The old man wouldn't hear of it and explained that he had another job he wanted to talk to me about and figured that we could do it during dinner. Laughing, he patted his shirt pocket and said, "I've got your money right here". Nodding in acknowledgement, I figured that even though I was going to have to eat, I wanted to hear what he had to say. Work was slow and if being his guest at dinner would get more work, then it was worth my time.

We sat down at the table and I realized the old man had planned this in advance. There was a place already set for a third person and since it was just he and his wife and now me, I was somewhat puzzled. Regardless of the feeling that was going through my mind at the time, I figured having me to dinner meant he wanted to try and get me as cheap as possible on the new job he was going to talk about.

He began by explaining that his pond out front needed to be somewhat deeper, and the cattails growing inside needed to be dug out. I didn't remember seeing any cattails earlier and continued to listen about how he wanted it done. I explained that I could probably do the job and we continued eating our dinner. The fried meat had a different taste than what I was use to, but the flavor was a good one and I thoroughly enjoyed it.

I agreed to drive back up the next day and look over the job he needed done and meet him later to discuss the pricing. He said that he would be in town working on a house and to look him up at home later that evening. He never asked where I lived or my name. I felt obliged not to question him the same. On my drive home I thought about the man I had just met. Who was he and what was a poor old carpenter doing with a podium in his living room?

The next morning I drove back out to the old man's, parked on the road leading to his house and looked out over the pond. Like so many roads in Warren County, it was a lightly traveled blacktop road. Anyone who drove up could go around my truck with ease.

Looking toward the old man's house I saw the dog which could pass for a brown bear. I didn't feel like trying the damn dog and he didn't look too eager to come down to the road. He appeared to be content to sit on the opposite bank and watch me. Technically, I wasn't in his territory.

The pond was, at one time, nearly an acre. Now it had largely filled with mud and cattails so that there were gently sloping banks of mud running into a small, probably shallow, pool of brown water. The old man said there were some man eating catfish in it, and that he wanted to save them. To drain the water, push the mud out and shape the banks would take several days and I wondered whether the old man could afford it.

When I spoke with the old man later, I recommended a money saving alternative. He could hire someone with a large bull dozer to push the mud out and I could use a smaller bulldozer to customize the banks. It would be cheaper overall and I wouldn't have to chance getting our little dozer stuck in four feet of mud. He said that he would get back with me and that was the last time I spoke with him for several weeks. During the interim, without my knowledge, I was thoroughly investigated by the Ku Klux Klan.

The old man eventually called. It had been such a long time since I heard from him that I had forgotten about the job. I figured that it was too expensive, so I was surprised. He explained that he had a friend push the mud out and wanted me to come back and look it over again.

The next afternoon I went to his house and saw an ugly one acre mud hole with no water in it. I explained to him that yes, I could fix it for thirty-five dollars an hour for as long as it took. I further went on to say that he could stop me whenever he felt that I had done enough to suit him. We agreed that I would start the job a few days later and work until it was completed. This was a big job and I decided that I would do the work myself instead of hiring an operator. That way, I would maximize my profit. I figured it would take about a month to finish. During that month, I would learn all about that old man.

It wasn't too long after I began working on his pond that people started showing up to watch. Whole families would drive up, pull out their lawn chairs, coolers filled with food and drink, and lounge around watching the bulldozer. At times, the front yard had so many people you would have thought it was a family reunion. The drive was lined up with cars all the way back to the road. His children and grand-children, as well as other relatives and friends would all drop by and watch for several hours at a time. I learned that his relatives owned all the land around and on both sides of the road. I realized then that the old man had a lot of family and friends, a lot more than anyone else I knew.

I had been working on the pond for a while when one evening the old man came out to watch me. Sometimes he would do that when no one else was around. He was standing on the bank of the pond holding two cold beers and I took that as a cue to shut down.

As he was handing me one of the beers, he said, "I want you to come to a special community meeting as my guest on Wednesday night." He proceeded to explain that it was an informal meeting to discuss issues affecting all of us and would be held at his house. Jeans and a shirt would be the attire. Not finishing our beers together, he turned and walked back to his house with me standing looking confused. A special community meeting? Be his special guest? Well then, I would come and maybe I would finally get to learn about his podium.

Chapter Three
Attending a Meeting

On Wednesday night around seven o'clock, I guided my truck down the old man's gravel driveway. In a line beginning near the road to the left of the drive were several cars and pickups parked end to end all the way to the house. I could see lights glowing through the windows from inside, but no one came out to greet me. I didn't see anyone, let alone the man who was standing in the shadows of the corner part of the house.

I parked behind the last car, turned off the engine, opened the door and stepped out onto the grass. Quickly, in long strides I advanced to the door and knocked. It was opened immediately and I faced for the first time a fully robed Ku Klux Klansman. He was eight feet tall, as wide as the door frame itself, and glaring at me through two hideous eye holes. I froze.

Far away, as though I was in a tunnel with only the sound of my heart beating out of my chest, I could hear someone say, "He's okay, let him in". The man's eyes softened and he motioned me inside. I had never been as scared as I was at that moment.

As I entered into the living room, there were even more of them, maybe twenty in all. I had to keep telling myself to calm down, that this wasn't the end of the world. I heard the door slam shut behind me and I felt as though I had just walked through the door to another dimension. Quickly, I walked over to the wood stove on my left. With eyes that were as wide as golf balls, I looked around the room again. I wondered if they could sense my fear and if so, what would they do to me? Some people were looking curiously at me and others were arranging chairs for sitting. When one of them offered me a chair, I almost fell to my knees. Sitting down as quickly as possible and trying not to look as though I might die of a heart attack right then and there, I was relieved that at least I would be closer to the floor.

Looking around again, I noticed that every one of them except for one was dressed in white robes from head to toe. Some had on pointed hoods with the facial covering pinned back, while others had no hoods on at all. The sole exception, completely robed in black was the only one whose face I could not see. He peered through two dark, round holes at me and the glare was so fiery, that I felt as though my head would catch fire. I turned away and tried to focus more on the surroundings. I noticed that in the corner of the room there were some assault rifles. A lot of them had gunslinger style holsters with guns in them. I just couldn't make anything worth while out of the surroundings and felt as though something was going to happen although no one seemed to be agitated. Everyone was milling around engaged in separate conversations as though they were at a Halloween Costume Party. But this wasn't Halloween, nor a party, and I sure wasn't going to pretend that it was.

A man sitting at the table next to the podium began calling the roll. As he called out a name, that person answered *"Akia,"* whatever that meant. After the roll was called and everyone answered accordingly, the old man rose from his seat and slowly walked up to the podium. The room fell silent. He motioned for me to stand.

Rising on rubber legs, I stood and he began talking, "We have a special guest with us tonight. Some of you may recognize him from working on my pond." I noticed several of the men glancing at me and I sat right back down with a thump, hoping no one else heard or felt it. I was thoroughly embarrassed. The old man went on speaking. He welcomed his fellow brothers and thanked all for coming. He explained that he wanted to talk briefly about the local political situation.

Trying not to squirm in my seat like a child in school, I listened to the old man talk about how time was approaching to start some fund raising and campaigning through the summer which would help with the fall elections. Raising his voice, he went on to say that the political scene in Bowling Green was rotten and now was the time for a change.

With the voice of a good old Baptist preacher firing up his congregation, he denounced the local county judge executive, the mayor, and a local circuit court judge. He went on to say that they were corrupt and must be toppled from power. They were extorting the working man with taxes to pay for their extravagant lifestyles and that we, the working man, are paying for it. His voice boomed and cracked thunderously.

"We shouldn't pay their damn taxes," he roared, pounding the podium to emphasize each syllable. "The goddamned Jews are backing them, international finance Jewry," he bellowed. "It was the Jews who pushed taxation all over the world to bleed wealth from the common, hard-working, decent folk so the politicians could pay interest on Jew loans." It was the Jews, he continued, "who financed the Northern war against us and freed the Negro to forever remain among us as a disgruntled and hateful race of misfits, always looking for us to pay them reparation for bringing their savage asses into the civilized world. And it was the Catholics who joined with the Jews in early Rome, and had lain with them like fleas on a dog ever since to exploit the industrious Anglo-Saxon race, a race of men who fought against the swords and armor of imperialist invasion with sticks and field rocks, and bled the ground red with courage." The room exploded with applause.

"Unless we want to lose the future for our children, we must always stick together and remain united," he spoke quietly, in whispers, like a man who had lost his only son, and to great effect, about the need to preserve America for Americans. "Without us to hold the torch of freedom, the flame will die and all the blood poured into the grass of battlefields here and around the world will have been in vain."

The old man had spoken for about twenty minutes when he stepped aside and asked a man to speak about a local family for whom donations were needed. It was an impoverished family who had suffered a house fire and was living day to day in a motel. They needed food, clothes, furniture, and money for rent. He described the children and some of the sizes that they wore. Canned goods were best, just a can or two of anything that anyone had to spare. They had a car, but gas money was a problem, and the father was willing to work in the evenings and on weekends for anyone who could afford to pay him. Did anyone need any yard work, cleaning, painting, carpentry, or handyman work done? The message was clear enough; help if we could. He told us to get with him after the meeting, or call him at home, to donate anything of use. The *Kleage* had the information and the man sitting at the table nodded in agreement. Some of the Klansmen promised to provide some of the things that the family needed as well as giving the father work. As I listened to the discussion, I felt extremely proud to be sitting among these people.

The old man stepped back up to the podium to let everyone know they were planning a rally and a march in a small town in Tennessee. It was to be a membership drive for a newly formed Klavern. He explained when it would be and when he would be leaving to drive down. He offered to take anyone who needed a ride and to lead the other cars down. No one asked any questions and I received the impression that they had done this many, many times.

The meeting ended with the old man giving a short prayer. There were refreshments in the kitchen, including sugar cookies and iced tea. The Klansmens who still had on hoods, with the exception of the man in black, removed them and began to talk amongst one another. The black robed man quietly slipped out the front door unnoticed for the most part, and did not return. I didn't hear a car leave however, so I knew he was out there doing something in the darkness. No one talked to me so I just stood in the corner by the stove looking stupid until the old man finally wandered over and asked me how I liked the meeting. I liked it a lot and he knew it. Feeling more than a little awkward, I begged his pardon to go. I would see him the next day when I arrived to do more work on the pond. With that I left, dumbstruck by what I had just experienced.

Later, alone, I reflected deeply on the night. Everyone there had been ordinary, hard working people that I might meet on any given day. It could be in the market, gas station, or just passing down the street. These weren't militant warmongers. They weren't bloodthirsty savages, salivating at the opportunity to go out and hang a black man. They were compassionate country folk who were interested enough in their community to meet to talk about it and try to do whatever needed to be done to help with it. Although they scared the hell out of me, I had to admire this group of people. My impression of the KKK was rapidly changing.

Chapter Four
Sign Me Up

I had returned and was working on the old man's mud-hole when he approached me about going to the march. Still nervous and unsure of what keeping company with these people might mean, I declined. He didn't seem too surprised. It was obvious that he wanted me to join and at that time I couldn't understand why. I have never done a thing in my life for anyone, much less the community. Why would they want me as part of a socially conscious group? I was a young punk out hustling money to spend on beer, marijuana and girls. What good was I to a group of men, such as the Klan?

The day of the march came and went and I finished the pond. By then however, the old man and I had developed a friendship and I continued to come to visit him. One evening he formally asked me to join and I explained my concerns that if people in the community knew that I was a Klan member it could subject me to heat from the police. He wanted to know why I felt that way.

I had begun fencing stolen automobiles, trucks and heavy equipment and didn't need any unnecessary attention. He assured me there would be no problem, that I could become a silent member. There were many members that no one knew, he said. There was no paperwork on them and their names were known only to a select few. I would be forbidden to tell anyone I was a member and could never appear in public, or even at meetings, in a robe without the face mask down so that no one could identify me. This alternative plan piqued my interest and I told him I would think it over, but in my mind, I knew that I was already going to join. I had no idea what a mistake I was making.

Just like everyone else who joins, I had to fill out an application, although after it was investigated by the Grand Dragon, it would be burned so that no written record of my membership would ever exist. In fact, I had already been investigated. I would have to take the oath and I wouldn't be required to attend meetings or any other gathering. I would be available to help any fellow Klansman if I was asked. I would be a member, but not an active member. I would be a part of the group, just top secret and accessible only to the top echelon of the organization. This secrecy appealed to my need to stay out of sight and I felt like it was the perfect option for me.

My entry into the old man's Klavern went virtually unnoticed. The only meeting I ever attended without my required disguise was the first one at the old man's house and I only attended as a guest at the time. None of the members would ever know that I was a Klansman.

The old man administered the oath at his home during a private sitting in his living room. I sat in a chair while he sat on the couch directly opposite. A low coffee table separated us. First, I was required to recite the oath which all Klan members must take. Normally, this was done while kneeling before a cross, however we skipped the formalities.

"Put your left hand on top," he said, gesturing at the open Bible lying on the coffee table, raise you right hand and repeat after me." I did as I was instructed and repeated these words:

"I do solemnly swear that I will support and defend the Invisible Circle; that I will defend our families, our wives, our children, and brethren; that I will assist a brother in distress to the best of my ability; that I will never reveal the secrets of this order of anything in regard to it that may come to knowledge, and if I do, may I suffer a traitor's doom, which is death, death, death, so help me God, and so punish me my brethren."

After all was said and done, I was shown a few of the secret signs and codes by which I was to communicate.

The handshake came first. If I suspected I was meeting a member for the first time or if I was meeting someone who proclaimed membership, I was to shake the normal way with one exception. The right hand index finger was to be extended over the other man's palm and against the inside of his wrist. If he did not return this gesture, I would know that he was not a brother Klansman. In a crowd of people, I would recognize other Klansmen by watching their right hand. If it crossed their right breast to grip their left coat lapel with the thumb and index finger, that would indicate they were Klan. There were many other variations of these gestures for each Klavern, but for now I would learn the universal ones.

When speaking on the telephone and I was unsure of the person on the other end, I could say *"akay,"* pronounced *"uk-kay,"* which meant, "a Klansman are you?" The person on the other end of the line would either ask "What?", or say *"akia,"* pronounced *"uh-ki-uh"* with a long 'i'. It meant "a

Klansman I am." Through the years I would learn more, but for now what he showed me was enough, lest I forget these things.

I left the old man's house feeling more than a little impressed. I was now a part of one of the oldest secret American societies and I was a top secret member.

CHAPTER FIVE
Learning Some History

As the weeks came and went, I continued to visit the old man often. I had a thousand questions about the Klan, yet I paced myself and only asked a few so as not to aggravate him. Sometimes, I would just ask something simple and listen, anticipating his answer. If the old man felt like talking, he would ramble on about the Klan and between fits of anti-this and anti-that propaganda to which I paid little attention, I learned a little.

The Klan began after the Civil War in order to stop the Northern government from completely taking over the lives of the Southern people. Even though the North had won the war, their intent was to remove every semblance of Southern culture from below the Mason-Dixon line.

To fight this, the Klan was formed. The North was using the blacks as pawns in an effort to project power into the South. Doing so violated the Constitutional preservation of states' rights. The federal government was using the excuse that the blacks needed protection from the whites, education, and assistance, in order to implement laws permitting federal agencies to exercise power over local law enforcement, commercial establishments, elections, and schools; all the centers of civil authority and power. The Klan saw the results of this and sought to persuade the newly-freed blacks not to go along with the Republican Northerners who were trying to implement these unconstitutional power grabs, and to vote for the Democratic politicians running in the local and state elections. The Klan believed the Democratic candidates were opposed to further federal expansion into the conquered states. When the blacks agreed, and most did, they were helped with jobs, food, and clothing. Since most of the blacks were former slaves of the very people who had joined the Klan after the war, there was at the time, no animosity between them. The blacks needed help and the Southern whites were providing it to those who wanted it. The problem began when the Northern carpetbaggers and

Southern scalawags convinced the blacks to promote the Republican pro-federal intervention measurers. This would inevitably prompt the Klan to attack the instigators and any blacks who followed their logic.

The second Klan, as the old man called it, began in the early 1900's as a result of immigration policies which permitted immigrants to take jobs from the American people. It attacked the bad points of industrialization, and encouraged the tightening of the borders to ensure Americans and their children would always have jobs. The Catholics and the Jews were responsible for giving away the rights of the white people. Their efforts were attacks on Protestantism. The Klan believed the white man should have the best jobs since they had worked hard to found America, and died fighting to protect it. This information provided by the old man could be instantly attractive to the hard working middle-class white in the early twentieth century.

It was during the second Klan, the old man said, that the Klan had its largest following. All the different groups were consolidated under a central management structure and things remained that way until the early sixties. It was called the *Invisible Empire of The Knights of The Ku Klux Klan.*

In the early 1960's, as part of the civil rights movement, a woman in California filed a lawsuit against the *Invisible Empire*. According to the old man, this suit threatened to subject all the assets of the Klan to possible loss from any judgment. A decision was made to break the organization up into separate, autonomous Klaverns. In that way, if any one Klavern found itself in trouble, the loss would be limited to it. All the members of the old Invisible Empire became Imperial Wizards, Grand Dragons, or other officers in these separate Klaverns, and that is how the third and final Klan began. It remains so today.

To skip forward in my narrative some, I later did some studying of my own on the Klan and some deep reflection on my past with them. I cannot deny the history as I learned it then nor can I deny the history as I have learned it now. Wrongs have been committed to the whites and blacks and others all throughout known human interaction. We can cry over these or we can learn and do better. I tell you this, however: before you can learn from history, you had better know the truth about what really happened in the past. My studies about the Klan, post Klan, were revealing and lent great understanding to the roots of so many of our transgressions against each other that I feel compelled to share it. Here is a very brief summary:

Ku Klux Klan is a distortion of the Greek word *"kukios"*, meaning circle, and of the word used to identify the tribal groups of families present in Britain before the Roman conquest. The name translates~ to "Circle Klan." The history of the Klan goes back to the Piedmont and mountain areas extending from Virginia to Mississippi, north of the so called Black Belt, to just before the end of the Civil War. Before the Klan, there were numerous protective societies among the predominantly Scotch-Irish whites who had organized to protect themselves from militant blacks who had been organized by the infamous Union League. These groups, such as the White Brotherhood, the Constitutional Union Guard, the White League and the Pale Faces, merged with the Knights of the White Camellia, who were the dominant white force within the Black Belt, to form the KKK. Each was formed as a defensive organization to restore social order in the midst of the unrest caused by the war. They drew historical examples from European groups:

The Carbonari of Italy, the Tugenbund and Vehmgricht of Germany, the Klepts of Greece, the Nihilists of Russia, the Masons in most Catholic countries and the Illuminati.

Six Confederate soldiers in Pulaski, Tennessee, several of whom were college educated, met in the fall of 1865 to formally organize the Invisible Empire of the Knights of the Ku Klux Klan. Contrary to popular history, the formation was a most serious affair, and would have as much influence on the future of the South as had the war itself. The problem which prompted this defensive response was the black insolence north of the Black Belt. Northern carpetbaggers, through their Union League, had organized black groups and taught them that lands occupied by whites should be divided up amongst them in repayment for slavery. They taught the black man that all the white wealth had been gained from black labor and should be returned, by force, if necessary. The majority of the black race, however, was peaceful by nature and it was difficult to rouse them to violence. Nevertheless, the Union League's teaching engendered a deep hatred in the younger blacks for the white man, and this hatred manifested itself in outright insolence, vandalism, and sporadic outbreaks of violence. The Klan was organized to resist the efforts of the Union League, not, as popular opinion would have it, to fight the blacks.

The struggle wasn't really about black rights. It was about power over Southern agricultural production and wealth. If the carpetbaggers could rouse the blacks to violence it would prompt their swift massacre by the majority whites — all of whom, unlike the blacks, were well armed with weapons from the recent war. If that occurred, the Northern government would be obliged to step in, take control of all civil institutions, and protect the Negro from extermination. With that control would follow total control of agricultural production in the South, the key conflict of the war itself. The blacks were pawns in a great game of manipulation. It was for this reason that the Klan remained a secret, as opposed to a public movement. It took a covert organization to fight a covert war, and between 1865 and 1871, the Klan won that war completely.

In 1871, the Northern government enacted the Ku Klux Klan Act and funded more federal assistance to the efforts of the carpetbaggers and scalawags. By then, however, the Klan had achieved it's goal of stabilizing communities in the South so that whites and blacks could live, separately, but equally. The need for which the Klan was called had gone, and it disbanded only to meet periodically to review the status quo and plan for the future. They would not appear again as a serious force until the "Roaring Twenties".

A preacher named Simmons, together with a quick witted marketing guru, reorganized the Klan to combat industrialization and immigration in the 1920s. In order to establish a strong financial base, they made a fundamental change to the former organization. They introduced a public membership that had never before existed. They promoted openness of identity and purpose. This was never a characteristic of the first Klan, but would persist forever as a legacy of the second. Now there existed a public membership, easily led, who joined for prestige. They paid dues in the millions, and there can be no serious question that this allowed the Klan to grow to be a powerful political force.

The descendents of the secret circle of the first Klan remained intact, but unseen, throughout the period of the growth of the flock of ignorant followers. They became known as "silent members", and when the curtain fell on the 20's, they would be there to pick up the pieces and carry on the protective struggle into the civil rights era, and beyond. Although I didn't realize it for many years later, it was this group to which the old man belonged, and it was to this group I was offered the chance to join. These were the ones who accomplished their objectives by threats and violence as a first resort, not a last one. It would prove to be the single biggest mistake of my life.

I identify the invisible Empire members, who were all in their fifties and up, as the Circle. These were the men of power — the ones any aspiring young man would need in order to gain rank. The ones whom I saw attending the meetings openly, and who were involved in the Klan as a social adventure, I refer to as the "Flock". The others, who stayed hidden and acted without talk, were the "Silent Ones."

Chapter Six
Gaining Trust

I continued to visit with the old man at his home even though I did not attend the weekly Klan meetings. Toward the end of the summer I was there one afternoon watching him bush-hog the field beside his driveway when his tractor quit. At the time, I was sitting in my truck resting, so I got out and walked over.

"Goddamned tractor," he mumbled as I approached. He was looking absently at the engine. "I need a new one. This thing breaks down damn near every time I use it." It was an old John Deere tricycle type, with two front wheels directly under the front of it, rather than out to the side. They were notorious for turning over on a hill because of the narrow front wheels.

"What kind of tractor do you want?" I asked him. He knew that I was in the business of fencing heavy equipment, and wasn't surprised at the question. I didn't have to tell him it would be hot.

"Well, I need one a little bigger than this" (his was about a forty horsepower), "but I don't want a new one. People would notice it. How much would a used one cost?"

I had made many sales like this over the past year, always to the farmers who couldn't afford the price of a new or used piece of equipment that they really needed, It made me good money on the side, and did them a favor. Since I acquired only equipment that I knew was insured against loss, I felt the loss to the individual dealers was minimal. No doubt, that didn't make it right at all, but it helped me justify my crime. I had a thing for insurance companies anyway.

I told the old man that I could get him one for two thousand dollars, and he could write out a receipt from a fictitious person. It would come from at least fifty miles away so that it would be unlikely that anyone would recognize it. He agreed, and I promised to deliver it within the week. Meanwhile, we pushed his tractor out of the field, walked to the house and popped the top on a couple of beers to seal the deal and cool down.

When I left, I called one of my associates to see if he was available to do a little work. He knew what I meant, since we only did one type of work. I drove out to meet him the next afternoon.

I met Troy when I was in the eighth grade. Unbeknownst to me, I had been out with his sweetheart who lived down the road from our farm, and he called me to tell me about it. Of course he wanted to fight, and I agreed to meet him at the local school yard that evening to settle the matter. He didn't show up, but I would eventually meet him the next year at high school.

By then, he had forgotten the girl and was with a new one. I met his older brother, Bill, first, and eventually was introduced to Troy. We hit it off immediately. It would be through his father that I would first enter the dark world of stolen equipment. Because Troy had the guts to steal and was able to learn how to operate various types of tractors and trucks quickly, he became one of my best sources for hot equipment. By 1988, he had become a true professional thief, and when I had a special request for something, I always called him first.

Troy was five feet, nine inches tall and weighed two hundred pounds or so, with curly brown hair and a pug face. He was the consummate country boy, complete with ball cap, red wing boots and flannel shirt. He was also a smooth talker, one of those who could talk faster than you could possibly answer, so he would just answer himself and keep right on talking. He was a lot of fun to work with.

He was always riding around smoking pot, looking for equipment sitting in places from which it could be stolen. He knew exactly where a good used tractor could be obtained.

He knew of an old farmer down the road from his house who had a good used tractor in his barn. Troy felt he could get it without any problem. He said the old guy was a real ass, had been arrested for beating his wife and kids, and deserved to lose anything we could take. I tended to agree with that reasoning. He said he would steal it and drive it to the old man's place for three hundred dollars. I told him to set it up, and agreed to go along with him in order to prevent anyone else from being involved. The real problem was that it was only about twenty miles from the old man's place to the farmer's tractor, a little too close. We would have to disguise the tractor after I delivered it.

The next night we set out to do the job. The tractor, a Ford 60-horsepower or so was parked in the barn we had just passed, Troy said. It was an old plank barn which sat about thirty yards off the road, just beyond a barbed wire fence. The fence row was grown up with small trees and bushes, making it hard for anyone to see from the road. A gate, located off a narrow lane connecting with the road, opened to a one-acre lot just behind the barn, and it was through that opening that we decided to bring the tractor out.

Since it was an area little known for tractor thefts, we expected the keys to be in it, even though I brought along a set to fit it just in case. The only problem was the proximity of the barn to the farmer's house. He would hear the tractor start that close. Because there was a slight grade from the barn to the road, we would have to push it uphill to the gate, then push it down the road before we could start it and drive off. That meant I was going to have to help.

I parked my truck a mile or so up the road in a thicket where it couldn't be seen by anyone passing by. We walked back to the gate, ducking in the ditch whenever a car passed. Standing at the gate, I looked out over the darkness for any sign of life. Nothing. We climbed the gate and ran to the barn. Before entering, we listened to see if we had awakened any local dogs. I hadn't seen any, but you never knew. I put my ear to the cracks between the boards making up the barn's front doors to hear if anyone was inside. Nothing. Troy pulled up the wooden latch, and we ducked inside. The tractor was there, pulled in so that the rear of it now faced us. Troy checked it, and the keys were in it. He pulled off the fuel cap and shook it to assure there was enough fuel to drive it away. It wouldn't need much, but I had brought five gallons along just in case. I opened the doors as he released the parking brake, and we started pushing it out of the barn and up the hill toward the gate. I was the first one to see the movement from the side of the barn. It was a large dog, but it wasn't barking.

"Troy, look," I whispered. He turned as the dog crept closer. "Hey man, that's a big *fuckin'* dog!" he whispered back. He was clearly getting nervous since he was the closest to it. "Give me the gun, goddamn-it," he said.

"Just stay still boy," I whispered. "Lets see what he does." He wasn't barking and wasn't running, and I wasn't at all sure that he was any less scared than we were at that point. I could always shoot it if it turned violent, but no use in being hasty. The dog eased closer.

"*Damn-it, boy, gimmie the gun!*" Troy was very agitated now. It was, in fact, a big dog. "Shut up, fool. Don't panic. Be still." The dog took a few more steps toward him.

"If the son-of-a-bitch bites me, god damn-it boy, give me the *fuckin'* gun!" Now, he was climbing on the tractor. The dog was to the tire eyeing Troy curiously. I was beginning to think it couldn't bark at all.

"Get back down and pet it," I urged Troy.

"Are you *fuckin'* stupid? Fuck you, I *ain't pettin'* nothing, shoot the bastard before it bites me!"

Well, this wasn't going to work. I started to call the dog to me. Its ears perked up, and it began to trot around to my side of the tractor. It stopped a foot or two away and sniffed me from a distance.

"I told you, you *dumb-ass*". Troy had found a hammer in the tool box, and was waving it above his head.

"Don't do it!" I said firmly. Too late. The hammer struck the dog in the rear-end. It yelped, ran off about thirty feet, and started barking viciously. So much for stealth.

"You stupid son-of-a-bitch," I said. "That dog was harmless. Now look what you done." I was livid. I started walking toward the dog, calling it in a soothing voice, when I heard a door open at the house. It was a screen door, one that hadn't been oiled since the battle of Shiloh from the sound of it.

"Shut up, Jake!" I heard a man from the house say. The dog kept barking. I looked at Troy, who by now had made it to the gate and was waiting to see what I was going to do. I knew what he was going to do: run like hell to the truck. I motioned for him to be still.

"Come here, Jake, its okay, here boy", I continued to softly call to the dog while watching the house.

Whoever it was hadn't shown any interest in leaving the porch over a barking dog. I hoped the guy would assume it was barking at an animal, not tractor thieves. The dog stopped barking, and stared at me. I eased closer, steadily whispering to it. I searched my pocket for something I could feed it, but I had nothing. I kept easing closer. It stood there, watching me.

I heard the screen door close as noisily as it had opened, and I realized then that this night would be successful. The dog must have sensed the end of the tension as well, because it let me walk right up. I began to pet it and apologize for my stupid friend.

We pushed the tractor through the gate and the dog escorted us down the road to where we started it and Troy drove off. I said farewell to the dog, walked to my truck and headed out to catch up with our new tractor. I drove ahead to the old man's house, woke him up to receive his machine, and waited with him for it to arrive. In about an hour, from the old man's porch, I saw Troy coming down the road, two yellow lights on the tractor fenders flashing brightly, like he owned it. The old man was incredulous. Troy pulled in the drive, shut off the flashers, pulled it around behind the house, and shut her down. I said good-by to the old man, loaded up in the truck and took Troy home.

I returned the next day to get my money, in cash. "Like it?" I asked him.

"I got a friend says he needs one too, *'cept* he wants a new one. Think you can get it?" he asked. I could, I answered. My fencing operation was about to take a new turn, right down Klan alley.

CHAPTER SEVEN
The Tompkinsville Pipeline

I began stealing in earnest when I was sixteen years old. I had been working for a construction company, operating a bulldozer, for fifteen dollars an hour, and decided to buy a new truck. The Toyota dealer agreed to sell me the truck as long as I could get a cosigner, which I had, and insurance, which I didn't have. I went home and began to call insurance companies, and to my surprise, I couldn't get insured. Since Kentucky law required insurance, and the dealership required full coverage, I couldn't buy the truck without it.

Most of the companies I called simply refused to insure me at any price. Others would do it, but at three thousand dollars a year or more. That was more than my payments on the truck!

I stewed over that unfairness for the rest of the day, and that night I went back and stole the truck. Of course, after joyriding in it I had to abandon it. I certainly couldn't keep it and I didn't know where to sell it.

Thus, my short career as a thief began.

Since I had worked in the area and spent hundreds of hours riding with friends at all hours of the night all over the region, I knew the schedule of the police and the general attitude of the community to late night oddities. This made stealing a cake-walk.

In the outlying areas of the city, there were several equipment dealerships selling tractors and other farm machinery. None of these places had guards, fences, alarms, or any security devices other than security lights. I didn't believe any of these devices would have mattered much in any event, since I would have circumvented them. There is no question, though, that their absence made my efforts much easier.

I focused on farm equipment because I knew where I could sell it. Demand dictates what is to be supplied, and there was no reason to steal something I couldn't sell, and sell at a good profit. I could sell small tractors for a couple of thousand dollars just about anywhere. That was good money for a night's work in your late teens.

To reduce the risk, I trained some of my high school friends to drive the tractors, showed them how to steal them and paid them anywhere from two to four hundred dollars to steal them and drive them to a place of my choice.

I wouldn't tell them where the tractors were going, just in case they got caught and decided to tell. They might be able to tell on me, but they could never tell on anyone else. If they told on me, it was their word against mine that I was involved, not a strong case for a prosecutor without some cooberating evidence. This was the method I used almost exclusively.

At first, buyers were sporadic. Whenever I was working in the county and met new people, I would look to see if they had a need for farm equipment. Only a few were ever reluctant to buy something stolen, and when I brought it up to most, they readily agreed to buy if the price was low enough. The problem for me was that I was essentially retailing by acting as my own salesman. This limited the number of buyers to just a few one-time purchasers since no one would need more than one tractor or bush hog, or whatever. Sometimes I would get turned on to a friend of a first time purchaser, and on one occasion, I found the opening to a major pipeline for stolen equipment.

Troy's dad, Bill, lived outside of Tompkinsville, Kentucky in a red brick house just off the two-lane state highway leading into town. I met him through his son. Troy said his dad knew a man that could use a new three-quarter ton four wheel drive Ford pickup truck, and would pay three thousand dollars.

"Where's it got to go?" I asked Troy.

"Tompkinsville. Dad said we could drop it off behind his house", Troy answered.

"Where in the hell is Tompkinsville?" I asked. "It's about a couple hours away down the back roads. *Ain't* no cops, *'cept* every now and then a State Trooper might cruise through. They never stop though. It's in the sticks, boy. *Nothin'* but dope, guns, and four wheel drives," he finished.

"When they want it?" I asked.

It occurred to me that I had never stolen a new Ford truck and didn't have the slightest idea how to hot-wire one. "You know how to get one?" I asked.

"*Fuck no*! I figured you'll find a way," He replied. Great. Three thousand dollars was a good lick and I had no idea how to make it.

We decided to drive down to the Ford dealership in Bowling Green and look at one as if we were going to buy it. At least we could see what kind of tools we would need. The salesman was more than happy to let us test drive a brand new blue one, and didn't even ride with us! He just handed me the keys and said take it for a drive! Troy and I looked at one another; we were thinking the same thing.

We climbed in, started it, and drove straight to Wal-Mart. I parked the truck, handed Troy the keys and waited while he ran in and had an extra set of keys made.

When he climbed back in, we slapped hands, kissed the extra set of keys, and thanked the god of trucks for blessing us.

"Nice truck, but I don't think I can afford it right now," I explained to the salesman when we returned; "Let me save up some money, and I'll be back." Sooner than he knew.

"Should we do it tonight?" Troy asked as we drove off in the Ranger. "Well, he saw our faces, and he knows what we're driving, but he doesn't know our names and he didn't write my plate down unless he did it while we were gone," I said. "I don't think he did."

"Fuck it, I'll do it tonight." Troy said. And that was fine with me too.

To kill the rest of the day, I decided to drive to Tompkinsville, meet Bill, and familiarize myself with the roads and the area. The road lay east of Scottsville, Kentucky, and wound through low rolling wooded hills, intermittently cut by small fields of grass and occasionally corn. At one point, we turned down a gravel "short cut" that Troy said would shave off several miles. I didn't know they still had gravel roads as long as that one was. It must have been over ten miles before we hit blacktop again, but I knew there was no chance of police presence along this route.

As we pulled in at Bill's, a large collie ran from behind the house to loudly escort us in. Troy jumped right out and began to walk to the door. The dog didn't pay him much attention, and chose to hang out by my door. Apparently Bill wasn't home and Troy got back in.

"He's out working somewhere and they don't know when he'll be back," he said. "Let's drive around the road to where we *gotta* park it."

We backed out, drove down about a mile and turned down an unlined one-lane road that ran through the area directly behind Bill's house. At a clearing, Troy motioned me to stop, and we got out. There was a single strand of electric fence held about waist high by small iron rods stuck every thirty feet or so apart. We stepped across and walked down the edge of the grassy field to a dirt lane that cut back toward the rear of Bill's house. After a few steps, I could in fact see the back of the house through the trees. It looked like a good place to park the merchandise.

"When are we *gonna* pick up the money?" I asked as we walked back to the Ranger. "When we drop it off!" he answered with enthusiasm, as if there was never any question about it.

It was well after dark when we returned to Bowling Green, and we swung by the Ford dealership to look the lot over again. It was still there. It was well past closing, and except for the hourly drive-bys by the city police, there was no security. There wasn't even a fence around the place.

"*Fuck it*, let me out," Troy said. I pulled over and he jumped out and began walking over to the truck. I pulled around to an industrial parking lot within sight of the lot and waited.

I was watching the entrance to the lot, expecting him to drive the truck out through it, when I saw a flash of blue bounce over the curb, through a drainage ditch and slide sideways into the road. Mud from the ditch was flying all over the truck and the road. When he straightened it up, I could hear the four-barrel kick in and saw the rear end slide sideways as he punched it, squalling tires. I pulled out to catch him and the race was on!

It was all I could do to keep his tail lights in sight all the way to the drop off point. I never came close to catching up. In fact, he had parked the truck - drove it right through the electric fence – and was standing on the road waiting on me when I pulled up.

"That *mother-fucker* will roll, boy!" he exclaimed as he climbed into the Ranger. He didn't have to tell me.

"Are you crazy?" I yelled at him. "Why didn't you use the entrance coming out of the lot?"

"*Fuck it*." he said, "I was in too big of a hurry. Besides, that's what four wheel drives are for, boy!" We laughed.

I drove around to Bill's house and rolled a joint while Troy went to the door. When he returned I learned that we would have to wait until the morning to get our money, so we drove into Tompkinsville, rented a motel room and waited.

When daylight came after a few hours sleep, we rolled out to Bill's. He was up, outside waiting. He was a short man, 5' 7" or so, with a pot belly, but not particularly fat. He was wearing overhauls and a coat, with a camouflaged cap that covered most of his straight black hair. I shook his hand as Troy introduced us, and I noticed that only one of his eyes looked at me while the other looked to the side.

"I trust that was what you wanted", I said. It was his cue to pay me.

"Yeah, it's a nice one. I *gotta* run over to get your money, but you can hang out here until I get back," Bill said.

He returned with thirty crisp one hundred dollar bills and laid them in my hand. "He said he can take two more of '*em* if you get '*em*," he said. Whoever "he" was had just made my day!

"Give me a couple of days," I said. "Where do you want me to take them?"

We climbed in his truck and he took us down the road to an old wood barn. We parked and a man at the house near it came out to greet use. "This is Hayden," Bill said as he introduced me. He was in his thirties, about my height and looked in decent shape. He showed us to the barn and told me to just bring the truck in at night and park it. The next morning I could come back for my money.

Hayden also asked if I wanted to buy some pot. Of course! We went in the house and in a back bedroom were maybe fifteen large black trash bags. Each one was filled with pot, not leaves, but good buds. I had never seen that much pot in my life! There must have been a hundred pounds of it.

He sold me a pound for a few hundred dollars, and Bill took us back to the Ranger. I had a pound of pot, well over three thousand dollars, and I could clearly see six thousand more in a couple of days. I thought I was *gonna* be the next John Gotti; yeah, right!

Troy and I discussed where we could get the trucks, and it was agreed that we should get them both at once, requiring a third person. We decided to locate the trucks and get the keys first, so we drove to a Ford lot in Russellville, Kentucky, south-west of Bowling Green to test drive a couple of Ford three-quarter tons.

The lot sat on a hill up off the road a mile or so outside of town. Further down the road was a Wal-Mart. The lot had no fence or gate to keep the trucks in, and we assumed there would be no night watchman. We couldn't be sure that: (1) the salesman wouldn't ride with us, thereby preventing us from making keys; and (2), that he wouldn't write our license plate number down and record our visit. To prevent, or at least deter the salesman from coming along, we relied on the fact that both Troy and me in the truck with the salesman would be crowded. The salesman wouldn't want to crowd us.

To prevent anyone from taking down the Ranger's plate number, I simply took it off and put it under the seat before I pulled onto the lot.

We test drove one, then the other, of two trucks, and made the keys before returning them. By now the thrill was over but I could taste the money. We thanked the salesman and said we would think on it. On the way back to Bowling Green, I told Troy that I needed to get another tractor and take it to the old man's house soon, and so we went looking for a tractor lot to kill some time.

CHAPTER EIGHT
Making Inroads

Troy knew a tractor dealership near Scottsville where he thought there would be no difficulty in stealing a new one for the old man. We drove out to look it over.

The weather had turned cold so we stopped by his house to pick up some extra clothes for him to wear. We arrived at the lot well after dark to find, as we expected, no one around. There weren't even any houses within sight. Although there was a locked gate across the entrance, there was no fence or other obstacle to prevent anyone from driving off with a new tractor. Troy wouldn't have any problem.

I parked the truck off the road and helped carry ten gallons of diesel fuel up to the lot with Troy. We picked out one of the new medium sized tractors and cranked it over to make sure the battery was up before we poured the fuel in it. We carried the fuel cans back to the Ranger and Troy bundled up for the long ride out to the old man's place.

Since he knew where we were going, I trailed way behind him, sometimes over a mile. I tried to just keep him in sight without being too close. If someone got wise and he had to ditch, I would know where he was to pick him up later without anyone knowing we were together.

Troy decided to cut through the outskirts of Glasgow, Kentucky, in order to cut off some time back to Bowling Green. When he pulled onto the bypass, a Glasgow city police car fell in behind him and hit the blue lights!

Damn! The area was urban – without much woods, meaning an escape must be made quickly, before reinforcements arrived. I waited and watched for Troy to jump and run but he didn't. He just sat there as the cop got out and walked up.

I could see the cop and Troy talking, with the cop standing on the road and Troy still sitting on the tractor. It was too late for him to run now, so I waited to see what would happen. No other police cars arrived, and that was a good sign. Then, almost as quickly as the stop began, it ended when the cop walked back to his car, turned off the lights, and Troy started to drive the tractor off.

I continued to follow at a distance until, several miles out of town, I pulled alongside and motioned him over.

"What the hell was that all about?", I asked as he climbed into the truck to warm up.

"He pulled me over because there have been several tractor thefts in the area. He was just checking me out. He laughed, "I told him I was just moving the tractor for my boss because we were *gonna* do some plowing in the morning."

"He didn't notice the new plastic still covering the seat?" I asked, incredulous. "Nope. He bought my story and told me to be careful," Troy said.

"Why didn't you ditch it to start with?", I asked. "Well, I figured if he busted me I'd go to jail and do my time and get out. *Fuck it.*" I couldn't believe what I had just heard him say.

"You're *fucking* crazy", I told him. He just laughed, climbed back out and drove off with his tractor.

We took the tractor to the field across the road from the old man's and left it. Rather than wake the old man, we drove to a motel in Bowling Green and got a room. Later that morning, I drove out to see the old man.

"The boy picked it up already. He'll bring the money for it by this evening", the old man explained. It was just as well. I went back to the room, where I had left Troy, and slept until it was time to go back.

The old man seemed really happy that I had delivered the tractor as I promised. Whoever his friend was had requested more.

"How many more?", I asked.

"I reckon he'll take all you can get. Said he'd be interested in a backhoe and dozer, too." The old man answered. The old man wasn't looking me in the eyes, which made me suspicious.

"I've got some stuff to do the next few days, but I'll get back with you on it," I explained. Troy and I left. We had two trucks to deliver.

Troy knew a young guy named Matt, who would help us steal and deliver the two Ford trucks. We picked him up and offered him two hundred dollars to follow us in the trucks to Tompkinsville, and he agreed. Since we would be back before the next night, there was no need for him to take any extra clothes, and we headed out.

We arrived in Russellville near midnight after stopping to eat and fuel up. Matt drove the Ranger, dropped Troy and me off near the lot, and waited up the road for us to take the lead.

We crept slowly up to the lot, watching and listening for any night watchman on duty. Certain that no one was around, we each got in a truck and the race was on when Troy squealed tires out of the lot.

This time, though, I had just as much motor as he did. I just hoped Matt could stay within sight.

We ran the back-roads as fast as we could go. We passed one another, jumped hills, slid around curves, and even cut through fields when the urge struck. We weren't stealing, we were playing, albeit dangerously, to be sure. When Matt fell too far back, I would flash my lights and signal Troy to slow down. Once he caught up, we would floor it again.

The three of us rolled in at Hayden's barn just as daylight began to break. We parked the trucks end to end in the main part of the center of the barn and closed the doors. I didn't see Hayden around, so Troy and I drove Matt home. I gave him two hundred dollars and some pot, and dropped him off. He had never spent a night out like that.

Troy and I drove straight back to Hayden's house. By the time we arrived, it was mid-day and we were tired. Hayden said that he needed us to drive the trucks down the road to another hiding spot. He seemed more than a little nervous, which made me nervous. Nevertheless, we agreed.

Along the highway there was the remnant of an old road that the highway had been made to replace. In several places, the old road cut down into the low valleys and disappeared in undergrowth. The whole area was under developed and wild with thickets and new growth anywhere there was not dense woods. Hayden pulled off the road onto one of these old road openings and waived us to pass him and drive ahead. I was leading, and what I saw made the hairs on the back of my neck stand up.

The road led down a steep grade from the highway. To the left was a drop-off to a creek bottom and to the right was the hill atop which the highway ran. On both sides were thick growths of small saplings covered with dense briars. The thickets began to coverage at the top of the road, forming a natural tunnel. On both sides of the narrow lane I began to pass parts of vehicle frames. Not old rusted ones. These were new! I even recognized the bed of the truck we had brought a couple days earlier. This was their chop shop!

I felt my stomach knot up. I looked back at Troy, and I could tell he was thinking the same thing I was: We weren't supposed to see this!

Instinctively, I felt the .45 in my back. Glad it was there. It probably wouldn't do me any good if this was an ambush, but I knew I could get off a shot or two. When you're young, you're bullet-proof and super-human.

I continued to drive until a new truck parked in the lane prevented me from going any further. There was no one around, and I had to assume the truck parked in front of me was freshly stolen also. I shut down the engine, left the keys in it, and got out. Troy was already walking back to Hayden's truck and I followed. As I walked, the place felt even more ghostly, almost as if it were a dumping ground for people as well as pickup trucks.

Hayden had to back all the way out to the highway. Back at his house, we waited for the money to be delivered so we could leave. We smoked a few joints, and drank a cold beer or two until a fat, gray-haired man in a four-wheel drive pickup truck pulled up outside the house and got out. We stepped out to meet him.

I met the man, whom we will call big Bob, as he counted out sixty crisp one hundred dollar bills in my hand. It was a large stack of money. I noticed he had on a large gold chain and large gold and diamond rings on both hands. I guessed him at around sixty years old. He didn't stay, and Troy and I didn't either. We were so tired, however, that rather than drive back to Bowling Green, we got a room in Tompkinsville and slept the rest of the day.

I remember thinking then that I had made it to the big league. In less than a week, I made almost ten thousand dollars. Of course, I had no idea what I was going to do with my life, much less the money. First thing was first: it was time to throw a party to celebrate my successful entry into the underworld. There was no place to go but up, or so I thought.

CHAPTER NINE
Shot Down In Cold Blood

Troy and Matt knew some college girls that lived in an apartment house near Western Kentucky University. Troy and I had returned to Bowling Green and rented a suite in a cheap motel on the outskirts of town. I gave Troy a third of all the money we made, less my expenses, and we started making calls to get a nice party together. In actuality, we had begun partying as soon as we checked in the room, yet we wanted to throw a big bash.

Troy was the social one and he knew all the party-goers to call. Matt set it up with the college girls to use their apartment and we set it for the next night.

I called a girl I knew, Katlin, and asked her to go to the party with me. Troy had picked up his truck, a new red Ford Ranger, and I had parked the doctor's Ranger at his office. I was quitting anyway. I had found a way to make much better money.

We left the motel the following day and loaded up on liquor and pot, and rented some movies to take. Troy and I were not dancers or romancers. We were drinkers and pot smokers, and we liked to sit and watch action movies. We lived for action – it was in our blood.

The party began early and in no time Troy and I found ourselves side by side on the couch watching an action film and smoking dope. I had a half gallon of Jim Beam and so did he. We were well into it when the people began showing up.

Because I didn't know anyone, Troy and Matt would tell the college girls who was permitted in or not whenever the door bell rang. One guy, a drug addict nick-named Fratboy who lived with relatives across the hall, knocked and asked to join the party. We were drunk and feeling generous.

Fratboy, I later learned, was a shooter – one who uses drugs intravenously – who hadn't been out of Kentucky State prison long. He was about five foot eight inches tall, maybe a hundred and sixty pounds, and generally appeared to be white trash. Not long after Steve let him in, there was some commotion in the kitchen area and Matt came into the living room where Troy and I were. The new guy, Fratboy, was talking bad to the girls, scaring them, and they had asked him to leave. He had refused and seemed to want trouble. I told Troy to go in there and forcefully ask him to leave.

When Troy came back in the room, I figured it was over. Not so.

"He says he *ain't* leaving," Troy said.

"Is that right," I answered as I rose to get on my feet.

"Look Brian, this dude *ain't* no joke. He's a big dude and he's on that shit," Troy warned me.

"On what shit?", I asked.

"He's a shooter, boy. He's crazy," Troy said.

I could tell Troy was scared. Odd, I thought. Here was my friend, fearless in the face of an arrest and jail, yet scared of this punk junkie. "I'll handle it," I said as I headed in to see Fratboy.

"Listen," I began, "this is these girls' house and if they don't want you in here, then you're *gonna* have to leave." He just looked crazy at me. Okay.

"Maybe you don't understand," I began again. "You *gotta* leave, now." I was right in his face.

"*Fuck you*," was all he said, and I hit him. We rolled around for a minute or two until I got a handle on him and put him out the door and locked it. No big deal – where's my drink?

Not to be.

Katlin, who had been hanging out with me at the party, was mad now. I guess because I had fought to protect the college girls. Who knows why, but she wanted to leave. Because it was dark, and we were in a bad part of town, I walked her out to her car. She opened the door to turn on the interior light and look for her keys as I stood by the open door.

Troy's truck, in which I had arrived, was parked only a few feet away. I had left my pistol under the passenger's seat because I didn't think it would be appropriate to bring it in the house during the party. It was a politeness I would never make for anyone ever again.

From out of nowhere, a hand grabbed my shoulder and spun me around. "I'm *gonna* kill you," was all Fratboy said as he pulled the trigger on a .38 caliber revolver which he stuck in my gut. Instinctively, I pushed him off of me and made for the house. A shot or two went off behind me, but no more hit me.

I felt the pressure of the bullet as it went through my stomach, and by the time I made it in the house, I could feel the burning. It was like a red, hot iron poker slowly pushing all the way through me. I knew I was going to die.

Luckily, one of the college girls was in nursing school. She took control, laying me on the bed and began to administer first-aid.

She probably saved my life. As I lay there, staring at the white plaster ceiling, I thought about how young I was, and about all the things I still hadn't done. She was screaming at me, "Breathe Brian! Breathe!" But I couldn't. Slowly, I drifted off to sleep. No dreams, no nightmares; nothing. Oblivion was the only thing in my sight.

I was operated on for several hours. It was touch and go for me. My family, as well as friends, stayed during the whole ordeal. The outlook wasn't so good according to the doctors. Only time would tell.

Miraculously I did survive the operation and was on my way to recovery. In fact, I didn't realize how close I'd come to dying. After the operation, they put into intensive care for several days with a twenty percent chance of survival. The future was still bleak, and the road to recovery was a long one.

A couple of weeks later, I learned Troy knew the guy had a gun at the party but was too scared to tell me. He was gone somewhere, on the verge of insanity so everyone said, and no one knew where he was. I felt sorry for him, knowing how he must feel, not knowing if I were going to live or die over his mistake.

The shooting and its aftermath ended my activities for several months. It would take weeks to get off the pain medication, and years to rid myself of the problems which one single bullet caused.

CHAPTER TEN
Meeting My Nemesis

During my recovery, I stayed with my parents on their farm. Just down the road lived Randy and Tesse, two brothers whom I had known since grade school. They were several years my senior and their life was one continuous party. I enjoyed hanging out with them, smoking pot and bullshitting about any and everything. Since I was supposed to be resting, I often hung out there.

One evening Katlin and I stopped to catch the two brothers in the midst of a small on-going party. I was, of course, welcome, and since Katlin was with me, I decided to stay. Soon, other people started to arrive, and Tesse decided we were going to need more beer to accommodate them.

An attractive blonde, five foot seven with a very nice build offered to take Tesse and I to town on a beer run in her car. I had never seen the girl in my life, and didn't think much about her offer at all. I must have been really naïve back then.

Half-way into town, Candi, which she said her name was, asked Tesse and I if we would like to come over to her place for the night. I was shocked, but I didn't object when Tesse said we would.

Back at the party, I told Katlin I was going to stay with the brothers overnight and she should go on home without me. No sooner than Katlin left, Tesse and I were in his car headed for Candi's apartment in town.

We went in and sat on the couch watching TV for a while before Candi went upstairs. Tesse and I stretched out on the couch and started to catch a nap, when Candi came back down the stairs and asked me to come upstairs. Just like that, we became lovers.

She explained that she had known of me for years and wanted to get to know me since she first saw me. She knew a hell of a lot about me, especially who all my friends were and what I had been doing. She was a mystery to me, and at first I was attracted to that. Yet there was something about her that I could not understand which made me uncomfortable, even defensive, with her.

I left Kentucky the next morning and didn't return for several months. When I returned in the late Spring, I was fully healed and functional, though I had to watch what I ate. Slowly, I began to regain my physical vigor.

It was the old man who, upon my return, told me who Candi was. She was a member of his Klavern's "Youth Corps", and was the boyfriend of a former Grand Dragon. Apparently there had been a problem between the Grand Dragon and Candi, precipitating their separation. The old man assured me, however, that they were still intimate.

Candi made allegations that the Grand Dragon beat her up. These allegations were brought before the Klavern, and he was, so the old man said, kicked out of the Klavern. A new man was filling his position temporarily, but the old man was looking for someone permanent.

Candi had more history than I guessed. I wondered if she knew my connections with the old man. I naively concluded that it would be impossible for her to know that and dismissed the thought from my mind whenever it arose. In this, I critically underestimated the law enforcement community.

Candi was gutsy. After testing her in a few minor legal infractions, I could see she had nerve and could be useful to have around. Troy was gone for the most part, and I needed another close partner like him. She was there at the right time to fill a void, another coincidence. Though occasionally I felt something was wrong with her, I put it out of my mind probably only because we were lovers. Anyone else I probably would have avoided entirely because of such suspicions.

I continued to shun any public role in the Klan despite subtle urging that I attend various events. Because of the thefts I was involved in, I was ducking all attention from any source. The less people knew about me, or saw me, the better off I would be.

I visited with the old man frequently, however, and I also continued to supply both him and Tompkinsville with tractors, trucks, and now back-hoes and small bull dozers. I had recruited a new crew for these efforts, though I still occasionally permitted Troy to move things through me when he was desperate. He couldn't sell to anyone on his own because no one wanted to deal directly with him. They would only deal personally with me. I suppose the general reluctance to deal with Troy stemmed from his unreliability. He never did what he said he would, and people quickly tired of that. He had also gone way downhill following the shooting.

I had taken Candi along on a few ventures over the summer also. Some for the old man, and some for Tompkinsville, She thus knew what I was doing and the general area where I was doing it, but I never let her meet anyone. Her role was always limited to that of a lookout or driver. She learned the faces of some of my crew of thieves, but I was careful that she never knew their names or where they lived. That caution proved itself later on.

Candi showed herself to have intelligence as well. This was probably the most important thing I liked about her. She had the ability to learn quickly, take instruction well and under pressure, and critically, to anticipate accurately ahead for what needed to be done in many situations. If she was unsure of what to do or say, she had the brains to do nothing and say nothing until she was sure. These qualities were highly unusual in a woman of twenty years of age.

The real problem was: she was an informant for the police.

Chapter Eleven
Volunteering To Act

The old man was leery of Candi and troubled by my relationship with her. Although she was never present during any conversation between us, she did accompany me a few times on deliveries and money pick ups. She would wait in the vehicle when these things took place, but she knew what was happening each time.

Nevertheless, the old man looked to me to implement strategic objectives for the Klan in a silent capacity. Though I couldn't know for sure, it seemed clear that all the equipment I was running to him was being dispersed through members in a wide area. My reputation among them grew rapidly as a dependable and active covert operator, and that naturally led to the next step in my career.

The old man brought it up in a very casual way. A member was having a problem out of a guy who didn't want to pay for some work the member had done on the guy's house. Would I be interested in helping out with this problem?

The government would later say that I turned down this road because I wanted to keep the old man from cutting off my fencing pipeline through the Klan. I couldn't agree. I did it from a sense of loyalty and honor among thieves and among fellow Klansmen. Money always motivated me, but only directly. I hadn't learned then how to make money indirectly.

In fact, there was nothing for me to consider at all. I volunteered to handle the problem strictly upon the old man's assurance that the member was worth the effort. If he was important enough for the old man to mention it, he was important enough for me to help.

One Saturday morning I met the old man at his house and he and I drove to the residence of the problematic guy. When we turned towards Tompkinsville, I started to get a funny feeling. I had never considered there to be a link between this old man and Tompkinsville. But why not? How could I have been so ignorant?

As we passed by first Bill's house, then Hayden's, then the chop shop turnoff, I never said a word nor even looked from the road ahead. Was the old man giving me some kind of message? I couldn't be sure.

Eventually we passed through Tompkinsville, on the outskirts of which we passed a one-level red brick house where the old man said the guy lived. We turned around a little further down the road and passed by the house again. Then we drove back to Bowling Green, the entire trip taking up most of the day.

I was told not to kill the guy or seriously maim him, just scare him into making the payments he owed. The method was left to my discretion, and I decided that I would forcefully encourage the guy on a personal level rather than burn his house down.

The entire trip to T-ville (as we called Tompkinsville) had left me a little rattled. I didn't know who lived in that red brick house, but I had met several people in that town, particularly in the middle of the night in some remote areas. I could very well know someone who knows him, I thought, and he might identify me if he got a good look at me. That meant I would need a disguise.

I visited the old man to tell him my plan. Since it was for a member, why don't I approach him as a member, in a robe and all, and scare the hell out of him? The old man thought it was as good an idea as did I. I would need a robe since, at that point, I had never had any need of one. The old man said he would loan me one and went to a box in the corner of the room to retrieve it. He said it would fit, and I opened the box to look at it.

It wasn't white, it was black!

"It's the Grand Dragon robe," he explained. "You can borrow it for awhile." Good God! I knew the Grand Dragon position was vacant and I was deeply concerned about wearing that robe. Yet, how could I refuse?

The house lay in a depression off the narrow road surrounded by woods. Across the road was an open grassy field fenced in by three strands of barbed wire. There were two other homes a few hundred yards down, but nothing above or across from the guy's house. I couldn't tell from the drive-by, but I assumed there lay a patch of deep woods directly in back of the house. It was isolated.

Because the house sat in a depression, I chose a place behind and to the right in the woods on a small elevation to stake it out. I needed to know the guy's schedule and how many people lived or visited there. I found a road on the topographic map from the county clerk's office that lay about a mile in back of the house, drove along it to find a good place to park my truck as if I were a hunter, and made the short hike overland to the placed I needed to watch from.

I took a knap sack with some food, binoculars, a buck knife, and extra socks in case I had to get my feet wet somewhere. It was well into the morning when I cleared a place to lay and begin my stake-out.

There was a pick-up missing from the driveway by the time I got there and I had to assume the guy had left already. I would wait until he returned.

The old man said there was a woman who either stayed there or was around there a lot, and I assumed the Ford Escort parked in the driveway was hers. She might or might not be inside. I waited.

Near noon a pickup pulled in and a man got out wearing blue jeans, work boots, a windbreaker, and a camouflage ball cap. I saw no dog or other animal come out to greet him. If he had animals, they were inside. He went around to the back of the house and entered the only door I could see other than the front door. He stayed maybe thirty minutes, came back out dressed the same. He got in his truck, backed out and left. It was time to take a lunch break.

As I started to eat, I heard the back door open again and a middle-aged woman came out wearing tennis shoes, jeans, and a long coat. She had long curly black hair and was slightly overweight. She entered the Escort, started it and let it warm up a couple of minutes before backing out and leaving also. She took a purse so I figured she was going into T-ville for something.

What this taught me of most importance was they only used the back door to come in and out of the house. This made things much easier.

I waited out the rest of the day, watched them both come home around five o'clock and didn't see either of them leave again before I hiked back to my truck in the dark. I still didn't know a lot, but I knew more than I did earlier in the morning. What I really wanted to know was the time he left for work. If, as it appeared, the woman slept late – as most women do who don't work – I could catch him coming out of the back door without involving her.

I decided to stay the night rather than drive back to Bowling Green. I parked a mile or so down from the guy's house early the next morning to watch him drive by. He passed by after daylight broke, yet before the sun was up. I guessed I would need to be at his back door at least thirty minutes before that.

I drove back to Bowling Green to get the things I would need and returned, arriving around dusk. Early the next morning, I took the plate off my truck and parked on the side of the road about a hundred yards down from his house. It was still dark. I stuck my .45 in my pants, pulled the robe over my clothes, and with a Louisville Slugger in one hand and the hood in the other, I jogged down to this house and slipped into the woods just off the back door. After an hour or so, the door opened and the guy stepped out, shut the door, and walked quickly toward his truck. I eased closer, and slipped on the hood and face mask as he opened the truck door. The interior light beamed out. I just got close enough as he climbed in to stick the bat in the door before he could close it.

As soon as the door hit the bat, I jerked it open and reached in, grabbed him by the jacket collar, and pulled him out onto the ground before he realized what had happened. As soon as he sprang to get back up, the bat caught his knee hard and he went down. It was then that he looked up at me.

His expression went from shock and pain, to terror. He tried to say something, but nothing came out of his mouth. I hit him with the bat again in the shoulder, and he found his voice. "Stop! I've had enough! Don't' hit me anymore!" He gave up.

"You owe somebody some money and I expect you to pay it by the end of next week. If not, I'll be back," I said.

He nodded his head in agreement.

"Roll over," I ordered him. I wasn't sure if I'd broken his leg or his shoulder, but I had to be sure he couldn't run after me. I brought the bat down hard on his ankle, and he hollered. I told him to shut up or I would hit him again.

"Count to one hundred slowly before you move. My brother is watching from the woods. If you try to follow me, he will kill you." I lied. I eased back until I couldn't see him anymore, I took off the hood and sprinted back to my truck, started it and sped off in the opposite direction. So much for that.

CHAPTER TWELVE
Making Grand Dragon

I never knew the man's name, or how bad I had hurt him. I learned from the old man that the debt had been paid and he was grateful for the deed. When I tried to return the robe, he told me to hang on to it for awhile because, as he said with a sly smile, I might need it again.

I continued to move equipment through both the old man and T-ville. Candi and Troy were scarce and I only heard from them when they needed something. Otherwise, I never saw them. By this time, I had a steady girlfriend and was trying to settle down.

I didn't have to wait long before the old man found another job for me. This time, however, the problem was with a local judge. He was alleged to be on the take of the local click of politicians and county gangsters who ran drugs, prostitution and gambling houses in the Southern Kentucky region. It was rumored that he had even been caught with cocaine in his possession, though I could never verify it.

He was said to throw big parties – coke parties – with wild women at his house, and to have solid ties with the underground, whoever they were.

His biggest sin against the old man was issuing an arrest warrant for the old man's nephew. The warrant led to the nephew's arrest, where he was lodged in the local jail. A severe beating by jailors caused his nephew's death. The old man was livid. He wanted the Judge dead.

Before we could get that worked out, the "Timbo" affair – previously discussed – arose and I was appointed *Grand Dragon* officially, though still silent. I began to attend some, but not all meetings and other affairs in that capacity, though never without my hood and mask on. My identity was top secret, and to all observers, the old man and I were just friends.

The "Timbo" affair also brought me into contact with other people like myself. They were enforcers from other Klaverns and at each event I attended,

I would make a new introduction. The two who helped me with Timbo were from Tennessee. There were others from all over, and hundreds of them I never met.

They didn't know much about me, nor I them. Yet we easily recognized one another, even if we were meeting for the first time. I just knew by the look in their eyes, that impassionate yet fiery look that is so hard to describe. I guess its like pornography – you know it when you see it although you can't define it.

The only real problem I had attending these affairs officially was the perpetual talk about blacks and Jews. I have never been a bigot – one who hates other races – though I do prefer my own culture over others. Yet, the only thing the ignorant mass of members talked about was hatred of blacks and Jews. The old man never preached hatred, just preference and self-preservation. Nor did others like me even mention the subject. It was always something limited to the throng of uneducated folk who attended.

I was never asked my opinion during those years. I was content to let people assume what they wanted. My robe spoke for me – dark, secret, menacing. It kept members at a distance, and I encouraged them to keep that distance.

You might ask why was I even in the Klan if I didn't like that kind of talk. It is a legitimate question. I stayed for the sense of justice for all and for freedom of all against injustice dealt out by tyrannical politicians. Although I was a thief, I needed that sense of serving a higher purpose to justify my existence. I fancied myself as a savior, not a criminal. Such was the lack of my knowledge at the time. There are many others who are like that as well.

CHAPTER THIRTEEN
Learning Secrets

The Grand Dragon position is the second in command of a Klavern. To fill that role, I had a lot to learn. I was given a Kloran – the Klavern's book of knowledge – and unfortunately it has been lost to history. I have included a similar one in the Appendix, though ours was different in many respects.

The old man taught me how to wear my robe properly – belt tied on the left hand side, not in the center – and how to properly salute a burning cross. He lectured me on the philosophy of the Klan – to preserve America for the white race, and the overall objective – to rid our homeland of injustice, poverty, and the influence of inferior races who did not have the interest of white people in their agenda. The most important thing to know, however, was how these objectives were to be achieved.

We were organized for both security and effectiveness. At the lowest level was the general membership. For a yearly fee, white appearance, and regular attendance at meetings, virtually anyone could join. You received a card for your wallet certifying you as a member, and for thirty dollars, there was a tailor to sew you up a white robe and hood.

Although I was never a part of this group, I did spend time among it and can evaluate the primary characteristics of its members. Most were members of the low to middle income class – not poor, but not rich. Their educations were generally of a high school drop-out level or lower. Most were generous, caring people. To sketch them as hate-mongers or violent would be erroneous. They were people well-liked in their communities, even by the blacks.

Because I was raised in rural America, I only saw rural members. These were country folk, unconditioned by urban views of race and society. They were simple folk, with simple ways of life, and simple ideas about it. They worked hard, took rest at leisure, and tried to enjoy their lives unhurried by the quest for more and more money. Social status meant about as much as economic status to them – very little. Most probably didn't own suits or irons.

As one climbs the hierarchal ladder of Klan organizations, however, the picture changes. Those at my level were more educated and more worldly. They were always younger, perhaps not as young as I, but much younger than the top echelon.. They were idealists fighting for what they believed was their cause for existence. Passion and adventure characterized their motivation for everything. They were the 'movers and the shakers', the people who made things happen.

Then there were the Imperial Wizards – the old men. They were generally of the economic middle class and part of the 'landed aristocracy' of the local community. Normally, they would be politicians, and in every sense they had all the attributes of that nimble and smooth class. But politics were something they shunned.

There is a perfectly good reason for this. Although they promoted democracy, they believed in dictatorship. They were never elected, as one would suppose a high office in a democratic organization would be. They were, from the beginning, self-appointed. No one was elected by the general membership, they were appointed by the old men. So, although they spouted democracy, they ruled by dictate. Democracy was something of which they wanted no part .

Finally, there are those members of the silent kind, of which I have spoken previously, and of whom I always remained. It was always to this group that the serious business of the Klan – terror and political muscle – fell. The members of this group span all economic and social classes and remain always a mystery. As I have said, their numbers are significant but not great. The problem with tracking their number is the lack of records. Although an initial record is generated by a formal application and dues are paid annually, these records are destroyed and dues are simply deposited in the Klan treasury as anonymous donations.

It is true that the Imperial Wizards know who the silent members of their Klavern are, and it stands to reason that, if the number was large, some roster would be required; if one exists, I do not know of it.

I have always thought of the Klan as a three-part organization with the general membership as the lowest and least informed part. They supply the mass of public support and visibility, and it is toward them that all propaganda is made. Issues of freedom, race, religion, and social equality are fuzzy concepts for them so that those who have more fully formed these ideas can influence them. Politicians, preachers, television programs, and radio talk shows have a great impact upon them; just like the Klan leadership.

Adolf Hitler showed the world that even a deeply divided political mass of common folk can unite when these fuzzy concepts are made simple, clear, and easy to grasp. Americans are no more immune to this strategy than Germans – Simmons proved it in the Roaring Twenties with the Ku Klux Klan revival to millions of members.

The second part of the Klan is the silent membership. These people are not easily led. To the contrary, they are fiercely free thinkers, idealists, and rationalists. This quality makes them powerful – the trick is to have them exercise that power for, rather than against, a particular idea.

The third and most important part is the leadership.

This three-part organization promotes security by requiring a clear separation between the three. If, as is expected, someone bent on harming the Klan joins the silent or general membership, it would be extremely difficult for them to learn enough to do serious damage. As a silent member, I knew little about their activities on a daily basis though I knew many of the members. Had I made efforts to learn more, I would have been instantly suspected.

By the same token, the general membership knew nothing of me or my activities. The only link between us was the top leadership, and if it was bad, there would be nothing to save the Klavern anyway. Of course, that is precisely why Klaverns are no longer nationally tied together in any formal manner. Any Klavern can go bad without hurting the movement at all. That is the beauty of de-centralization. To destroy it is like trying to pin a ball of mercury to a flat table with the underside of a metal spoon.

Chapter Fourteen
Coalition with The Skinheads, or Not?

In early 1991, Troy began cooperating with law enforcement and I became the target of a 'controlled buy' of a stolen farm tractor. My best friend had set me up.

Troy had been hit and miss, as I have said, since after the shooting. Hard up for money, he had been seen breaking in someone's barn to steal an ATV 'four-wheeler' to sell to someone. I heard that he had been arrested and released on bail – nothing unusual for a first offense minor theft. But Troy had turned: he told the police he 'wanted out.' To do that, they said, he had to get me.

Within a week he was calling; he had a buyer for new tractors – one a week – in Indiana. I agreed to meet his 'uncle' – an undercover state trooper – and at first sight I knew he was a cop. He was unlike anyone I had ever dealt with, a little too polite, a little to refined, a little too *'city-fied'*

I called Troy's dad, Bill, to verify this 'uncle', and Bill assured me that not only was he legit, Bill had just sold him a pound of pot. Bill had been involved in my first forays and I trusted him not to lie to me. Against my better judgment, I decided to deal with them.

Meanwhile, the old man needed another tractor. I had long since stopped personally stealing anything. I relied instead on a small group of men scattered across the state for that. One of these was a man everyone called Dino.

I hired Dino to steal a Massey-Ferguson tractor from a dealership lot on the northern edge of Bowling Green and drive it to a drop off for later shipment to Tennessee. On the night of the theft, I had Troy with me – he was making sure to keep close tabs on me for the police – and he said he needed to call his brother to tell him he would be late getting home. At a phone booth, while I sat in my truck just a few feet away, he called the police to tell them where and when I would make my next move: tonight at the Massey-Ferguson dealership.

The city police maintenance building was right across the road from the tractor lot. I was nervous about it, so luckily outside of Troy's hearing, I told Dino that, rather than drive the tractor off the lot in the front, he should drive it off the back and cut through a patch of woods to hit another road. The police set up surveillance at the maintenance building.

Troy had a sudden urge to go home, so I dropped him off and drove by the maintenance building and the lot again. I parked just down the road to watch everything.

I waited several minutes after Dino drove the tractor off the back of the lot to see if anyone had noticed. I detected nothing. We delivered the tractor without a problem; later I learned that the police, expecting me to drive a tractor off the front lot, never saw it leave. They didn't notice the tractor missing until the next day when they counted them!

I, on the other hand, was visited early that next day by Troy and his 'uncle!' They want to 'buy' that Massey-Ferguson tractor. Too late, I explained, it's gone.

"Can you get it back?" the uncle wanted to know. "It's just what I want."

Little did I know he wanted it to save face on the royal screw up of their 'sting!'

I did check to see if it had left yet, but it was in fact, gone. There was nothing to do but get another one for the uncle.

Within a couple of weeks I eventually had Dino steal another tractor, and Troy and his uncle took delivery of it. They made sure to record me on audiotape, accepting payments and a week later, I was arrested.

I stayed in jail for over four months before making bail. Troy was the star witness against me, and the law had managed to turn Dino and many others against me. They had even turned Hayden from Thompskinville, who also turned on the old fat man, all based on the information Troy Hale gave them. The Thompskinville pipeline was shut down.

Within weeks of my release, I was back in business with the remainder of my crew – including Candi – only now I was moving semi-tractor trailers. I remained, also, active as silent Grand Dragon.

Because my new truck ring was focused in Eastern Kentucky, several hours drive from Bowling Green, I was out of town almost continuously. I would drive in a couple of times a week to see the old man and attend affairs.

In the fall of 1991, the old man said he had received an inquiry from a skinhead group who wanted to form a coalition with our Klavern. We agreed to hear them out and put the matter to a vote.

The skinheads were a neo-Nazi group originating in Southern California who espoused government overthrow and white dominance. This latter point was the closest thing they had in common with us. They were a dangerous group of radicals, prone to violence and victimization of society. One thing I will say for the ones I knew: they were well disciplined.

They wanted to throw a rally on the old man's farm, after which the Klavern would vote for or against entering a regional coalition with them. The old man brought the proposal up at one of the regular Wednesday night meetings, and as usual, everyone agreed to his strategy.

I knew next to nothing about skinheads. I found it funny that anyone who had a good head of hair would shave it; I had brown curly hair and wore it long. I couldn't imagine how stupid being shaved bald would look.

I knew also they were city folk, and I always distrusted city folk. They thought we country folk were dumb. They made fun of our accents and the way we dressed. I always had contempt for city folk, and skinheads were to be no exception.

The old man continued to discuss the Judge and his desire to kill him. Clearly, the matter had been side-tracked because of both other matters and my continued absence out-of-town. I was enrolled in college by that time and between chopping Mack trucks, attending class, and Klan meetings, I was running ragged. I wasn't too keen on killing a Judge anyway, especially for simply signing an arrest warrant.

But to the old man, it was much more. He saw himself locked in a covert battle with the local political click: it was war for him, and reluctantly, I had to agree with him on that point. The Klan was a target. Anyone who could bring it down would be a hero in the eyes of the blacks and sympathetic whites, and all politicians want to be public heroes.

To the old man, the Judge had to go because this was a war of survival. The only questions were when, how, and by whom would he be killed.

My Dad

New Barren River Baptist Church

The old man's house

Overlooking Bowling Green

CHAPTER FIFTEEN
The Rally

The weather was calling for rain. The rally had been scheduled for several weeks and couldn't be changed now. The old man and a representative skinhead decided to go ahead, hoping it wouldn't rain and if it did, it wouldn't last long. Both hopes were in vain.

I arrived at the old man's early to help set everything up. The day earlier, other members had constructed a forty foot long cross, made from two telephone-pole sized cedar tree trunks wrapped in burlap feed sacks. Diesel fuel was poured over it and permitted to soak into the sack wrapping and the cedar wood underneath. A four foot hole was dug in which to set and tamp it solidly.

A wooden platform was constructed towards the end of the field, in line with the cross, with a concession stand not far off to its left. The platform was four feet or so off the ground, with a podium and chairs resting upon it. Wooden steps led off either side.

A backdrop was attached to the rear of the stage that reached six feet or so higher, upon which were a Confederate and American flag and other symbols.

In the field directly before the stage sat two large speakers tied to a circuit control box, with another electric cord running to a microphone attached to the podium.

As we began placing metal chairs in rows facing the stage, the clouds darkened. It didn't look good.

We turned our efforts to setting up the cross. The old man had a small dump truck parked in the field and we backed it up to the end of the cross. The other end was placed directly in front of the hole we had dug for it. The cross was soaked in fuel oil, and anyone who handled it became contaminated.

The men worked together to put the other end in the bed of the dump truck, then stand with it as the bed was raised. After much effort, the cross was raised and set, then tamped in. It was a monster, casting an evil watch under a deteriating sky.

People began to arrive. We had a man standing at the road to wave people in and another one to direct parking in the field. The skinheads had begun patrolling the perimeter of the field with assault rifles strapped to their backs. I let that pass, since technically this was their rally. Normally, however, such a show of weapons is discouraged.

The field began to fill up with automobiles, and people were milling around in the field, looking at the cross, the stage, and obtaining hot dogs and sodas at the little concession table. It looked as if it would pour rain any minute, and some folks had donned rain coats, umbrellas, and ponchos just in case.

The old man stepped on the stage and motioned for the skinhead reps to take a seat with him there. As they did so, I noticed some commotion near the house. I could see a man with camera bags wrestling with a couple of skinheads for control of his bags so I hurried over.

"He doesn't want to let us search his stuff," one of the armed guards said.

"Why do you need to search it?", I asked.

"We think he's a cop," he answered.

I told the man to take his camera bags and go on over to the stage area. I explained to these knuckleheads that it didn't matter if he was a cop, we don't care who he is. It didn't matter since there was nothing illegal occurring and because everyone who needed to be disguised – including me – was. There were plenty of reporters here taking pictures, I pointed out, so one more photographer didn't matter.

Reluctantly they agreed. I also explained, or rather, instructed, that we don't search people at rallies unless we suspect they are armed, and then only to protect the leaders from a public assassination attempt. Yes, they may search people in California, but this is Kentucky and we do things differently.

This incident, as well as the overbearing militant approach these neo-Nazis made, would be significant in our later vote not to coalesce with them.

While I was occupied with this event something more important unfolded outside my presence. A preacher from the Baptist Church located just a few miles down the road had shown up with a video camera. When the guards saw this, they forced him to leave unless he left the camera in his vehicle.

There was a trailer park next to the field, separated by a grown up fence row, so the preacher left and parked at one of the trailers. He began to video tape the rally from there and one of the perimeter guards spotted him. The guard aimed his assault rifle at the preacher, prompting him to re-enter his vehicle and quickly leave the area.

I was totally unaware that any of this had happened.

Almost as soon as the old man began to speak, the rain began in earnest. People ran for their cars and others braved it under umbrellas. I just stood there, watching and was thoroughly soaked in minutes. Then, as quickly as it began, the rain stopped. No one knew for how long.

We decided to light the cross, since darkness was falling. On a clear night it would have been visible from anywhere in Bowling Green. Tonight, however, the rain ruled the night.

To my surprise, the cross lit and managed to burn while we circled around it and began to chant in rhythm, "White power, white power," louder and louder. Then it began to rain again. We saluted the burning cross as it fought the rain, and as the light of the fire darkened, we separated and filed toward the house – the rally was over.

People had been leaving continuously since the rain began, and what few remained gathered on the hard wood floor of the old man's living room.

"The devil was determined to stop this rally, but we had it anyway. We will never let anything stop the Ku Klux Klan!" the old man said. We all applauded, but we knew this had been a failure.

At the next scheduled meeting our Klavern met to vote on the skinhead coalition. After hearing the reports of what they had done and seeing how they conducted themselves, it was unanimously decided to vote no. The old man would deliver the message and I thought the affair was over.

Chapter Sixteen
Something Must Be done

After the rally in October, the preacher, who had been there, published an article in the local college paper denouncing the Klan as a "putrid cancer on the body politic of society." It was the first time I could recall anyone ever publicly speaking out against us in the local area. The college, Western Kentucky University, was located only a few miles from the old man's home and was always a helpful source of new recruits. That the newspaper would give the preacher a voice against us was disturbing to the circle.

A couple of weeks after the rally, the old man called me to an unscheduled meeting at his home. He said it was important that I attend, and I got the feeling after hanging up that something was wrong, though I didn't know what. I had not read the article, and had no idea what could have happened to warrant a meeting with me. In fact, I mistakenly thought it might be a trap, such was the state of my paranoia by then.

That fear always haunted me. I never knew when the forces of evil would come together and met out to me what I had given others over the years. When would the circle make the determination that I knew too much? When would some aspiring ass-kisser convince the old man that my usefulness was at end? Would I have any warning at all?

It was those fears that prompted me a few months earlier to set up an insurance plan. Not the ordinary kind – the kind that only the underworld uses. The idea is to develop strong relations with others who are in positions which are similar to your own. These people know the need for mutual protection from the people they are supposed to trust. You agree to back them and in exchange, they back you. In my case, I found Danny.

Danny lived in Eastern Kentucky, in the foothills of the Appalachia Mountains. He was originally from Detroit, Michigan and moved to the hills to escape a dragnet for him made by local drug dealers he had robbed.

At fifty years old, he reminded me of any politician one might run into at the local City Hall. Distinguished posture, gray hair, and always dressed in fine suit clothes. Not many people knew he was an alcoholic. Yet he was perfect for me, and I grew to like him as a brother.

Danny was a thief by trade, and that meant he was not a coward. He wasn't scared to run into a place and shoot it out which is exactly what I needed. If I were in trouble, I wanted a man who would act on impulse, and Danny would act. I gave him a sawed-off 12 gauge shotgun and made sure that he practiced with it. He was a little old, but with double-ought buckshot, he couldn't miss at close range. I showed him where everyone that could possibly ever hurt me lived and what they looked like. That included the old man. All I had to do was call and let him know where I was going and what time I would be back. If I didn't call him before then, he was going to come and get me. If I were dispatched, he was to kill every man, woman, and child he found on the premises and burn the place to the ground.

In exchange for this commitment, Danny gave me the information on some of his local political enemies and I agreed to do the same for him. For either of us, this insurance wasn't much, but it was all we had. The real effectiveness of it laid in the fact that all our potential enemies knew about our pact. Unless they could kill us together they couldn't be sure they would ever be safe from reprisals. It was just enough to keep everyone guessing. Just enough to keep my ass alive.

After the old man's call, I telephoned Danny and told him where I was going. "Expect me back by daylight the next morning," I said. I also cleaned and loaded my Colt .45, pulled on my camouflage jacket, and left for the unknown. I would come back or I would not. I never had much choice in these things anymore.

There were no introductions when I entered the living room of the old man's house, where all the meetings were held. I noticed several new faces and many familiar ones. There were the familiar Wizards and Dragons from the several Klaverns in Tennessee, Indiana, and Kentucky. There were also several faces that I did not know. All I received were nods of recognition from those I knew and hard stares from those I did not. The old man was growling about the article the preacher had written. He said he was tired of being slandered by his neighbors, and that it needed to stop.

I was immediately relieved that this meeting wasn't about me, though I wasn't sure what it was about. I was sure of one thing, however. This was not like any meeting I had been to in the past. For one thing, the only people sitting were old men, only some of whom I had seen before. All those standing were younger, and only some of them I knew. I inferred from this sitting arrangement, that those sitting were all Wizards and those standing were Dragons. I remained standing.

That so many Klavern representatives were here meant this was an important meeting. Everyone was dressed informally, as was always the case in these affairs. Some wore blue jeans, others overhauls. Flannel shirts were common, and everyone was wearing boots of some sort. For such an important event, no one would know by the dress.

As I listened, I quickly learned the meeting was about the article published in the college paper. A copy of it lay on the small coffee table next to the couch, and heated comments were directed at it.

"Who does this guy think he is?" someone said.

"Fine thing for a man of God to be saying", another chimed in.

"How do you think it will go over at the school?", one man asked. He looked like a 55-gallon drum on a sawhorse, wrapped in a patchwork quilt which he no doubt called a shirt. I only knew it was him speaking because his jowls were shaking.

"I don't think it will matter much to those kids," another voice answered. "If anything, it will only cause 'em to be curious about us. That's a good thing."

"Well," said a tall, thin main sitting on the end of the couch, something must be done to teach this guy his manners." And, with that, all seemed to agree.

The discussion turned to just what should be done. "We need to send a message to the community, especially the college, that we won't be slandered," said a man sitting at the end of the room. I didn't notice him before, and I should have. He was younger than the others who were sitting, though not by much. His blond, curly hair was neatly concealed under a stocking hat, making him look more like a thief than an Imperial Wizard. In fact, he did not look like he belonged here at all. He was just a little too clean cut, too professional for this group. He continued talking. "The guy preaches down the road from here, and that is his primary point of public contact. What he said in the paper he repeats there. Without his playhouse, he can't do much."

"Why don't we just hit his family?" a Dragon from Southeastern Tennessee said. I knew him. He was close to six feet tall, with shoulders any college linebacker would envy. The only response he received was hard glares. This wasn't a meeting for guys like he and I. Our input wasn't welcome.

"As I was saying before, without his church, he has no regular medium to put this shit out," the blond man continued. "Perhaps, with the loss of the church, the community would shun him as a trouble maker. They might find another preacher."

"I don't' know," said the old man. Up to now, he hadn't said much. "I think it could backfire. What if the community rallies behind him in revenge?"

"They might, but I don't think so," the blond man replied. "I think the community doesn't want any problems because of something the guy didn't need to do in the first place. Besides, we have to do something, and I think taking out the church is better than taking him out. What other choices are there?"

"Well, we could not do anything," the old man answered. "Why do we have to do anything at all?"

"I can't believe what I am hearing," another man interjected. Watching him speak reminded me of an old Archie Bunker show. He looked and acted just like Archie. Fat with gray hair and a big mouth. "Damn right we're going to do something. I don't know what, but something!"

Everyone seemed to agree with this last outburst, and the room fell silent for a moment. It was hard to argue with the blond man's idea. It sounded appropriate, and wouldn't involve hurting anyone – always a plus for public relations. "Unless anyone has another solution, I suggest we vote on this one. If you have some objections, speak now," the blond man said with the tone of finality. No one said a word.

With that, the fate of the Barren River Baptist Church was sealed. Little did I know, mine was sealed as well.

Because the church lay within the territory of my Klavern, I knew this decision would affect me. I would be asked to take some part, if not handle it entirely. Again, there wasn't much I could do about that.

The meeting broke up slowly without any further discussion of the church or the preacher. I mingled with some of the fellows from Tennessee that I hadn't seen for months, one of whom I'll call Jake. I had met Jake in Chattanooga in 1989 on my way to a rally in Georgia, and I liked the guy. He was a bit shorter than me, around five foot, ten inches with black hair and a mustache. Not a muscular man, yet not skinny either. He was the ultimate country boy, complete with the Skoal can ring in the back pocket of his jeans and the red wing boots of a true "shit-kicker." He seemed like a genuinely good guy, and he had a personality that everyone liked instantly. I often thought that I could trust him if necessary.

"How are things with you?" I asked him.

"I'm thinking about quitting, Brian" he answered. "There's no purpose to all this anymore. All we do is talk about the same shit over and over. No one has any new ideas. No one wants to do anything except bitch about how bad everything is. I'm sick of hearing it, man." I let him finish. "I mean, what is anyone doing to make anything better? Not a goddamned thing, that's what. For once I'd like to see someone actually do something, like, well, anything, *god-damnit.*"

I didn't voice my opinion, but I felt the same way. I think many of us did. The circle wasn't doing anything but spewing hot air while we risked our butts carrying out their revenge on anyone who they didn't like. Were they putting together any plans for the future? Not that any of us could tell. Was there any future for the Klan? It didn't look like it. I understood Jake completely.

After the meeting, I stayed late to receive my orders. The old man and I loaded up his old four-wheel drive Chevy and drove out to look at the church he would ask me to burn to the ground.

The Barren River Baptist Church was the central focus of a small half circle of two and three bedroom red brick homes. From their location atop one of several wooded hills making up a ridge west of the city, the houses commanded a view of the night lights of Bowling Green, which hovered on the horizon to grant the residents a constant sense of serenity. The community and the church, like the road which was their artery into the city, each took their name from the swift, muddy river that flowed west through the north of the city and beyond to a wild country of rocky bluffs and wooded bottomland.

On the same ridge, just a few miles away, along a narrow country lane, lay the old man's farm. In each place resided antagonistic forces that any careful observer could have predicted would one day clash.

The church had between fifty and one hundred members. Even the old man used to attend, though I didn't learn that until several years later. Some even said he was married there. The preacher, on the other hand, was a newcomer. He had only recently begun services, and naturally, with his arrival followed hard feelings between the church and the old man.

Like the houses around it, the church was built of red brick with an annex attached for Sunday school classes. At the top stood a tall steeple crowned with the cross of Christ, making the place seem larger than it actually was. In front between the building and the road, was a large paved parking lot surrounded by unfenced grassy fields. No trees were to be seen and in back, a large field began and extended several hundred feet to the edge of a narrow wooded tract. Just beyond the woods, was a bluff leading down to the river bottom. From any direction an intruder could be easily spotted.

"A brick building *ain't* easy to burn. You'll have to get inside to do it," the old man said as we made the third and final pass.

"I reckon it'll be locked at night, but I doubt there'll be alarms. If the neighbors' dogs don't give it away, I don't see any difficulty," I explained. In fact, the houses were too close and there were several security lights which meant whatever happened would be visible to any curious resident.

"People go to bed early around here so you can do it late at night or early in the morning." After pausing, the old man continued. "Do you need anything?"

"*Naw*, I can get what I need. I'll find some help and a fast car, since this *ain't gonna* happen on foot," I answered. The place gave me an uneasiness, but at the time I couldn't figure out why. "When do you want to do it?"

He didn't' answer for a long time. We were almost back at his farm before he spoke. Was he rethinking the entire plan? He had not been an advocate of this at the meeting and seemed uneasy. Was it his affinity to the building?

When he finally answered, he spoke unusually slow and deliberate. "Normally, revenge is taken swiftly to ensure, without saying, that everyone knows what it was for. But it's already been a couple of weeks, and it's awfully close to home. I think we should wait a couple more weeks in case the preacher might be on the lookout."

That was something I hadn't considered. "You're probably right. But I don't think he would be expecting something to happen over a statement in the paper, do you?", I answered.

"Yeah. We go back a ways. He knows what happens, and I think he might be on guard. I don't think he will expect us to go after the church, though. But you never know. Any of those houses could keep watch for him, but after a month, he would figure we weren't going to do nothing," the old main said. I felt like there was something he was holding back.

"Alright then," I said with some relief that I had more time. "I'll wait until December, when it's a little colder." Hopefully, I thought, the neighbors would have their windows closed and be less able to hear any sounds made by a break-in.

After the brief recon, I returned home to think the matter over. This wasn't something with which I was comfortable. In the past, I had been concerned with imposing justice, even if too harsh on occasion. Now, I couldn't link the burning of a church with anything other than domestic terrorism. It was a new role for me, and I was having some trouble with it. Was burning the church justified by a public comment made by the preacher? What were we doing? The only answer I could find wasn't comforting – terrorizing the community. For the first time since becoming a member, I contemplated refusing an order.

If I were to refuse, what would happen? I had never thought of that. Would I be kicked out, or worse? How could they afford to let me leave after all I had done? And with that question, I seriously considered for the first time, what my position really was. What had I done to myself? When

I joined, I never asked how I would get out if I didn't want to stay. I never even considered quitting once I had joined. That thought was one I lost sleep over.

I decided to go ahead with the plans for the arson anyway, without finally committing myself to actually doing it. I would cross that bridge later. The night of the recon I knew it would have to be a quick, in and out job, relying on speed to beat reaction time if the police were called. This precluded a walk-in. A fast car to use as a getaway was the only option. Keep it simple. Drive up, break in, set the fire, and drive off. Use a stolen car and leave no evidence. Late at night, it would look like a traveler simply stopped in to relieve himself if the arson didn't take too long to do.

Although one person could do this, I believed it would take at least two, possibly three. One person would have to set the fire, but it would take two others to watch every approach angle to be sure no one spotted what was going on. One could act as a driver and lookout by parking in front of the church with a good view to one side. The other one would need to stand at the other edge of the building to watch the houses on that side. The third person would also be needed to warn the arsonist if he were in danger of being caught inside.

I figured I could use Candi as a driver and a boy named Jack as the third person. Jack had been helping me steal semi-trucks and had seemed to be very interested in the Klan.

"How would you two like to become lifetime members in the Ku Klux Klan?" I asked them. We were taking a slow drive along one of the numerous roads in the country. Both nodded their heads in agreement. Candi and Jack had worked together several times under my guidance by stealing semi-trucks and heavy machinery, and had shown their ability for this type of work.

Instinctively, Jack asked, "What do you need done?" He was a beanpole of a boy, twenty years old with beady eyes and a long straight nose. Today, as usual, he was wearing jeans and tennis shoes, with one of his colorful tee shirts, this one black with Van Halen written conspicuously across the front. He generally didn't talk much, and that was his best quality.

"I need to do a favor for the old man," I answered. They knew who I meant. "That's all I can say right now, and I'm not sure it will even be done at all." And I wasn't sure that it would be. I might just as well plan my disappearance if I refused to do it since that is what would have to be done for my survival.

"When?", Candi asked. She always wanted to know when I was going to do something, like it was going to interfere with her plans. I thought at the time she wanted to know my schedule so it wouldn't disrupt her many rendezvous with lovers, including me. I would learn later that there was more to her curiosity than I suspected. Had I not been intimate with her, I may have sensed it sooner.

"It'll be a couple of weeks. I'll let you know when the time comes. I just wanted to see if you were game. Nothing risky, just some dirty work to make the old man happy," I told her.

I knew that I had the authority to recruit new members, and I felt it was time to bring in these two. They had proven their worth many times, and I thought they could be trusted. What better way to bring them aboard than with an initiation task?

After dropping them off at their homes, I drove back to mine and began planning my strategies once again.

To set the fire, a quick accelerant would be needed. Since it must be done from the inside, safety required that it not be too explosive, otherwise the fumes could ignite before the fluid, thereby burning the arsonist. That meant gasoline was out. I considered diesel fuel, but rejected it because it burns so slowly. I needed something faster than fuel oil, and safer than gasoline. My final choice was Coleman fuel which is used by campers in stoves and lanterns.

I took the time over the next few days to scout for a car, purchase four, one-gallon cans of the fuel that would be needed, and three pairs of black cotton gloves. If I decided to do it, at least I would have the things needed. If I decided not to, I hadn't spent much.

Driving along the outskirts of Bowling Green, I found a white Chevrolet Z-28 IROC that would be easy to steal. It was parked at an old service station that had been converted into a used car lot. There were no fences or rails to keep thieves from driving off with the cars. I would send someone to test drive it, take it to the local Wal-Mart and have a set of keys made. It would be returned back to the lot, only to be stolen later on that night. The lot owner might remember the test driver, but that wouldn't matter much without a name, since I would be leaving the car somewhere for it to be found and returned if everything went as planned.

The job itself wasn't as difficult as others I had done. In fact, it was comparatively easy. What bothered me though was the job itself. I have always believed that everyone had the right to worship whatever and in any way they choose. I believed that the Klan upheld that right also. Now here we were, planning to deprive our community of their house of worship as if we somehow had that right. I had heard of church burnings in the past, but never gave them much thought. I believed they had all been locations that were used to organize violent opposition to the Klan and other white communities by radical blacks.

The Barren River Baptist Church, however, did not have a single black member. It was an all white church of my neighbors. What had they done to us? Certainly not organized violent opposition, much less any opposition. They had simply inherited a big mouthed preacher. I thought killing him was the better answer to this problem. I had always favored surgical actions to remove the key protagonists of opposition, not this type of blind terrorism. What was next, burning the church member's homes? I didn't hate my community, much less the members of this church. I didn't know them and I never condoned terrorizing the community for any reason. What I was realizing was that I had become part of one of the oldest terrorist organizations in the world.

I concluded, nevertheless, that I would fulfill the Klan's request to burn the church and gave the old man a call to verify that they still wanted it done. I knew they did, but I had hoped somehow something had changed to cancel it. It hadn't. "It's a go," he said and the conversation was ended.

CHAPTER SEVENTEEN
Disobeying Orders

On Thursday, December 5, 1991, I sent Jack and a friend to test drive the IROC and have keys made. Jack had done this before so there was no need for me to accompany them. In a couple of hours, they returned with the keys, and we waited to make the theft. After dark, Jack and my friend left and returned with the car. I promptly hid it and we waited until I decided it was time to leave. Even at this point, they still did not know what we were going to do, or where we were going to do it. They just knew it would be that night. I was leery of disclosing my plans too early, even to trusted partners in crime.

Near midnight, I told them it was time. I grabbed my army coat, pulled on the gloves and headed out to the car. Heading towards the barn where I had hid the car, the only sound was the crackling of frozen brown grass under our feet. No one would be out tonight, a week night, and most would be in bed since Friday would be a normal work day.

I gave my pistol to Candi to place in the glove box and loaded the Coleman fuel in the back. I don't think, even then, they knew what I was going to do. They never questioned me. I started the engine of our stolen chariot and pulled into reverse to back it out of its resting place. White wasn't the best color car for this type of job, but it was the easiest one to steal and had plenty of speed. Who would suspect a white IROC parked in front of a church for a few minutes to be up to mischief?

I drove into the country to familiarize myself with the car, and to have another look at the church. I made several passes and noticed nothing unusual. No lights on in the church or the houses which surrounded it. A good sign. I also could detect no dogs anywhere, another plus. It was now or never.

I pulled into the lot quickly and shut off the lights. Even then, Candi and Jack didn't know what was happening. When I got out and removed the fuel from the back of the car, I think the reality began to set in upon them hard. I was going to burn down this church, right here, right now.

"Come on Jack, help me with these cans," I whispered into the car. "Slide over here into the driver's seat and keep a watch on the road and those houses for lights," I told Candi. "If you see anything, honk the horn twice and we'll be here." She looked like a deer caught in the headlights of an oncoming truck. "Hand me the gun," I said.

Jack followed me, each of us with two cans of fuel, to the edge of the building, and waited for my instructions. I gave him the gun. "Keep your eyes on those houses for lights and don't let anyone come up on me in here," I whispered. Just above ground level where we were standing was a basement window. I kicked it out and climbed down inside. "Hand me the cans," I directed. He did. "I'll be back in five minutes." I didn't think it would take that long to do what I needed to do.

First I made a quick walk through to assure that no one was there. I began in the basement annex, then went upstairs and entered the annex. No one. I went down the annex hallway towards the sanctuary. Upon entering the holy place, something stopped me cold. I was awed with a feeling unlike any I had ever felt. My nervous system shut down. "Don't do this!" it screamed at me. I backed out rattled, and returned to the basement. At that moment, standing there in the basement, I made a decision that would prove my downfall from the Klan. Though I didn't see it at the time, what I was about to do would grossly violate my duty, and would not be forgiven. I changed the plan.

Rather than burn the entire church, which meant going back into the sanctuary where the uneasiness overcame me, I decided that destroying the annex where Sunday School was held would make a more appropriate statement. The people, I thought, could do what they liked, but teaching their children that we were evil was wrong. I would burn only the annex to tell the church patrons not to let the preacher brainwash their children against us. It was my way of tempering the message we were making to the community, and avoiding the force in the sanctuary. I won't lie about it, I was rattled good. I had no way of knowing that the Klan didn't care as much about the message to the people as it did about the message to the preacher.

I looked around. The basement itself was barren of furniture and wasn't much bigger than the average living room. I didn't have a flashlight, but there was enough light from the security lights shining through the windows to permit me to see. The stairs coming out of the basement and into the hallway were the only wooden thing I could find in the lower part of the building.

I needed to set the fire as low as possible in order to burn everything above quickly. I sloshed two gallons of the fuel over the stairs and along the wall of the stairway. A fire also needs good ventilation to supply oxygen. The stairway fire would draw air from the basement window once it began, but the window was too small to allow it to burn quickly. If it burned too slowly, there was a chance the Fire Department could put it out. I went to the back door and found it to be unlocked. Rather than break another window, creating more noise, I simply opened the door. The neighbors might see, though I doubted they would.

I went back to the stairs, the fuel now having had time to soak in, and poured the last two gallons on the stairs and along a trail toward the door. I fished inside my pocket for the lighter. When I lit the trail, it began slowly burning along the carpet down the hallway towards the stairs where it quickly caught hold and flamed up. That's it, time to go.

Jack was looking back and forth from the broken basement window to the houses. When I snuck up from the other direction, it startled him. "Lets go. Grab these cans."

"That was fast!" he said.

"It'll be burning in there a while before it can be seen outside here," I urged. We put the cans in the back of the car and got in. I looked hard at the surroundings as Candi drove us away for any sign of neighbors turning on lights and becoming curious. No lights came on, nothing was stirring. Good.

On Friday morning at 1:35 a.m., we drove off. By 5:30 a.m., the annex to Barren River Baptist Church was in ashes. The sanctuary remained.

The old man was livid. "Why didn't you bun it all the way down!" It was more of a command than a question, as if I should go back and burn the rest of it. I had driven up to see him a few days after the fire.

"I set it on fire," I lied. "But they either put it out or it burned out. There wasn't much wood in the place."

The following Wednesday after the fire, there was another Klan meeting. I brought Candi and Jack as my guests. It had been agreed to admit them as silent members, directly answerable to me. During the meeting, Jack sat on the edge of his chair, and I don't think Candi was even breathing. Nothing was said about the fire. The old man set the date for their admission ceremony a couple of months away, though I never told them when. It was something they would never attend.

After the meeting, the old man pulled me aside. "No one is happy about this, but there *aint'* nothing else to do. What is done is done," he said. Clearly though, I had created bad blood.

Chapter Eighteen

No Honor Among Thieves

In March of 1992, I went to trial on the state stolen tractor sting. Troy Hale duly appeared and testified against me, ensuring my conviction. It was all over in two days and I was taken to jail.

Within weeks, someone called Crime Stoppers to report Candi's involvement in the church arson. At least that's how it was to be told.

Alcohol, Tobacco, and Firearms (ATF) agent Raymond Cooper located her the same day and asked her to come to his office to talk about it. He had a signed confession in a few hours, including both my name and a general description of Jack – she never knew his name, and the general area where he lived.

It took Cooper another week to find Jack, bring him in, and extract a corroborating confession. They appeared before a federal Grand Jury on three occasions, precipitating an indictment of the old man and me. It was front page news, and at four o'clock in the morning of the next day, after the indictments were issued, a jailor brought the morning paper to me. "Is that you?" he asked, incredulous. As I read the article I knew that it was me and that someone had told.

That same morning, Agent Cooper arrested the old man. When asked if he wanted to talk, he agreed. Did he know anything about the fire, no. Did he know Candi, yes. Did he know Jack, yes. Were they members of the Klan, no. Did he know me, yes. Was I a member of the Klan, no. So far, so good.

Did he see me the night of the fire with Jack and Candi, yes. Were we in a white sports car, yes. Not good.

The old man and I had agreed that if it were ever brought up, I would claim to be out of town the weekend of the fire. His answers effectively hung me out to dry.

Agent Cooper never talked to me, and the one time he asked to do so, I declined to speak at all. I did not know who had told on me, and I fully assumed the old man would stick to the "script" – as government prosecutors would later call my alibi defense.

The Grand Jury also indicted my mother as a co-conspirator based on Jack's testimony that she knew what I was going to do. In fact, she knew nothing. It was a tactic orchestrated by Cooper to pressure me into cooperating against the Klan.

Bail was given to everyone except me. I would continue to languish, passed from one county jail to another, for over three years until the trial was finally concluded.

My family went immediately to work helping to prepare my defense. They collected witnesses, gathered records, and talked with the attorneys on my behalf. They didn't know whether I was guilty or not – nor did they care. They just wanted to save me. It was an effort that would cost much more than anyone could imagine.

The attorneys told me early on that if I would plead guilty, tell everything I knew abut the Klan, and testify, I would get a reduced sentence and the charges against my mother would be dismissed. Why wouldn't I do that, they wanted to know.

Honor among thieves is a difficult concept when one of them is telling, but no one knows who. I still didn't know who was telling what, or why. I was not permitted to see any statements against me, and would not until after the trial began. Did I think Candi and Jack were telling, yes. Beyond that, however, I believed everyone was sticking to the script.

I knew that my mother was innocent, and I was extremely confident that no jury would convict her. I didn't see her indictment as any real pressure – thus defeating the government's tactic. Also, the thought of telling on the old man was repulsive to me – he was my very good friend; I could never hurt him. I had no idea that he had betrayed me already.

As pretrial maneuvering continued, the government wanted to know whether or not I was going to present an alibi defense, and if so, they wanted to know the names of my witnesses. They had already threatened to prosecute anyone who helped me, and I was thus hesitant to give them this information. It was my attorney who did it before I could prevent him. His 'duty as an officer of the court' required it.

After receiving the names of my alibi witnesses, the rules required the government to give me the names of people they would call to refute my alibi – people who would testify for the government that they had seen me the night of the fire in Bowling Green. I received this list in the mail at the jail.

As I read down the short, ten or so, list of names, I saw those that I expected. Jack and Candi. and then my heart stopped. I blinked my eyes and read that name again. There must be some mistake. It just couldn't be.

But it was. The old man's name was there, a government witness. And just below his name was that of his son. It was not a typographical error. It was real.

I hurried to the telephone located on the wall of the jail day room. I had been calling the old man from time to time to discuss the case in coded language and he had never failed to answer. Since there was a recorded message preceding every call from the jail, anyone receiving such a call could hang up without accepting. That is exactly what the old man did that day. I never called back.

What had happened? I asked myself. What had I done to warrant this? How could he do that to me? An Imperial Wizard of the Ku Klux Klan, a rat? I just couldn't believe it.

Yet it had to be true. It was an official court document, and not only was the old man's name there, so was his son's.

All I had stood for – loyalty, trust, integrity, right vs. wrong – was gone. Little did I know at the time, I was the one who had been wrong, and wrong for a long time. My friends, first Troy, now the old man, had betrayed me. Of all the people, why them?

One thing was certain in my mind. I was determined more than ever to go to trial – to see and hear the old man, as I had seen and heard Troy, testify on the witness stand in front of God and country. If he was going to rat, everyone was going to know it.

The more I thought about it, the more important forcing The Old Man, Sr. to testify seemed to be. No one knew he was a rat. All the members and all the silent members – hundreds of people, many of whom I didn't know, had no idea. Because there was a lot of publicity on the case, the best way to prove to any and all was to force him to testify and make the paper and the five o'clock news. I had to go to trial.

This must have been a reaction opposite what the government intended. Rather than reconsider my refusal to 'cooperate', I had become even more determined to put the jury in the box after learning of the old man's intentions. Everyone in the case was now against me – Jack, Candi, Troy, and now even The old man's. All I had to do to skate out of it was 'debrief' on the Klan. And still I wouldn't.

I recall discussing this during a visit with my father at the jail on one occasion. I explained the situation and what the lawyer thought I should do: tell. My father looked thoughtfully at me and said: "Son, I wouldn't tell those sons-of-bitches a god damned thing!" I was never more proud of my dad. He had just shown more integrity than anyone I had ever met, and I knew he would always be my best friend.

Maybe the government was listening in on my visit that day, maybe not, who knows? It wouldn't be long after, however, they would apply maximum pressure at my weakest point.

CHAPTER NINETEEN

Pressure to Cooperate

Steve Kendal lived only a couple of miles from my family in Rockfield on the outskirts of Bowling Green. He was in his late thirties, early forties, with a wife and small children. He owned a two story home on several acres, and operated an electronics shop and sold satellite TV hookups.

He and my father had been friends for many years. It was that friendship which brought me into contact with Steve at a young age, and he became one of my first customers for stolen equipment. Steve was also a licensed firearms dealer and my supplier of guns.

When I first began buying guns from Steve, I was well under the legal age required. Steve knew that, but to evade the law, we simply didn't fill out any paperwork. If something ever came up, we agreed that he would say that he had sold the guns to my dad, and I would say I borrowed them from him. To further this strategy, I forged my dad's signature on a few transaction report forms and left them with Steve. He could fill them in anytime and back date them as necessary.

My dad was not aware of this.

Once I learned of the old man's betrayal, I began to focus on Steve as a key witness for my defense. Candi and Jack had turned over a gun they claimed I had the night of the fire and which supported a separate count of the indictment against me. The gun was one I had purchased from Steve Kendal.

I called Steve to let him know the situation and asked him to go ahead and fill out the form, with one caveat. Date it after December 6, 1991 – after the fire. He did so, and my dad went over and picked it up.

With a transaction form from a legitimate dealer showing that he had the gun until he sold it after the fire, I could blow Candi and Jack's story apart.

They were saying I threatened them at gunpoint to help me in the arson – a lie – and they needed me to have that gun at the time.

My dad gave the form to my lawyer to use as evidence. I told the lawyer, as I had told him about my witnesses, not to tell the government about the form or about Kendal. He told them anyway, and Agent Cooper promptly visited Kendal on the eve of my trial.

Kendal cracked under Cooper's pressure and agreed to cooperate. At last, Cooper had the pressure point he needed.

Under Cooper's guidance, Kendal told my dad the government had called him before a Grand Jury and he needed to know what to say. Unbeknownst to my parents, he was wearing a wire and recorded the conversation as my mother and father told him to just stick to the form, just say you sold it after the fire.

Indeed, Kendal testified before the Grand Jury, and four days before my trial was to begin, my mother and father were arrested under an indictment for obstruction of justice – soliciting Kendal to lie.

Agent Cooper personally sent a copy of the tapes to the jail and instructed the jailer to have me listen to them. Now surely, I would cooperate to free my parents.

As I listened to the tapes alone in an empty visiting room until late in the night, my will was broken. I went from disbelief, to anger, to raw hatred, then to fear, and finally to hopelessness. I was a broken child, and it seemed Cooper had won.

The lawyer was there the next morning which was on Friday. Trial was scheduled to begin on Monday. Had I listened to the tapes? I had. Did I know my parents were going to prison? I did.

"The government says they'll let them go, dismiss all charges against your parents, give you a significantly reduced sentence in a comfortable 'camp', just tell them what they want to know," the lawyer explained.

"I don't know what to do," was all I could say.

The judge released my parents on bond the day after their arrest. I called my dad over the weekend and told him what was on the table. Candi and Jack were telling. Kendal was telling. And even the Imperial Wizard was going to tell. What should I do?

Now I love my dad. "Son, I told you I wouldn't tell those sons-of-bitches a goddamn thing. Your mother and I will handle our own." He had just injected me with a healthy dose of conviction, and I couldn't have needed it more.

It was Monday morning, seven thirty AM and I was in the holding cell waiting to go into court. Everyone fully expected me to plead guilty, even my lawyer. He came to see me to get my final answer.

"What are you going to do, Brian?" he asked. "What should I tell the government?"

"Tell them to go to hell," I said.

Chapter Twenty
Betrayal At The Top

Press coverage of the trial was heavy. A Ku Klux Klan Wizard and a Grand Dragon were to face off with the United States and the entire community was watching.

The courthouse was an old three story block building sitting on the corner of Main and Center street in downtown Bowling Green. Inside, as is typical of older courthouses, the halls and rooms were huge, with high ceilings and marble floors. It was a place to accommodate large numbers of people. The courtroom itself was no exception.

As I entered it, I could see a large crowd both sitting and standing, eager for the show to begin. I generated silent stares, but no one seemed to recognize me – as I knew they wouldn't. The old man and his attorney were already there, sitting at one of two defense tables. We didn't speak.

The first thing everyone wanted to know was what I was going to do. The judge, John G. Heyburn, II, was a new appointee to the federal bench and had been informed of efforts to pressure me to cooperate. Since I clearly was not going to plead guilty, was I going to present an alibi defense or what? If I was, everyone – the government and the old man's lawyer, James McLemore could call and examine witnesses in a way to counter my defense. The judge asked me to personally declare my intentions, and I told him I was not going to do anything. I would just sit there and watch the parade of former friends tell on me and my family. I would buy their integrity at this trial, at an expensive price – the preservation of mine.

During opening arguments, when the attorneys explained to the jury what the case was about and what each party believes the facts to be, I learned for the first time what the old man's strategy was. If he was a government rebuttal alibi witness, why hadn't he plead guilty like the other cooperating codefendants, Jack, or received immunity, like Candi? (She had since married Tommy Patton, now deceased).

The old man hadn't pled guilty because he was hoping to escape punishment altogether. As his lawyer explained to the jury, he was innocent: I burned the church all on my own because I wanted to, not because he asked me to do it. The old man would "prove" that I did it and that somehow he knew nothing about it.

I now faced two prosecutors: the government and the old man's lawyer.

The government called the preacher of the Barren River Baptist Church, Larry Craig to the stand. As I listened, I learned that the old man and the preacher had a past stretching back twenty years. It seemed that Craig had been criticizing the Klan and the old man for at least that long as the editor of a newspaper in the neighboring county. He had only recently begun preaching at the church down from old man's farm.

He had gone to the rally in October of 1991 and had been kicked off the property by two armed guards, he said. And when he went next door to film it, one of the guards pointed a gun at him, so he left. He wrote a scathing article for the local college paper criticizing the rally and the Klan in general. That was the first time I learned what had happened at the rally.

Both Jack and Candi testified, describing the night of the fire and as many of my prior crimes as they could remember. They concocted one clear lie. They claimed they were both present when the old man thanked me for burning the church. This was a critical party of their testimony – it was the only direct evidence linking the old man to the fire. Without me, no one could ever say that I had been asked to do it, and no one knew what had really happened. The old man's attorney viciously attacked this part of their story, and rightly so. Everyone knew it was a lie.

Jack and Candi also testified that they knew nothing about the fire before it actually happened. Jack said he participated only because I threatened to kill him if he did not, and Candi said she didn't participate at all. I let them tell it their way.

The government brought Troy Hale into testify. He described my fencing operation with the old man and as many other crimes as he could remember. It was so nice to see him again!

Even the old man himself took the stand. He was the Imperial Wizard, he said, but I was not a member. He knew nothing about the arson. He did see me that night with Jack and Candi, however, so I couldn't have been out of town

I never took my eyes off him as he ratted on me just like the scurvy dogs who had testified before him.

To back his claim of seeing me, the attorney called the old man's son to the stand. He too, he said, saw me that night with Jack and Candi; his dad was telling the truth about that. Like father, like son, I told myself.

When it came my turn to present a defense, the judge wanted to know if I was going to testify.

I was angry after hearing the various lies mixed with the truth, everyone telling on me, but lying to protect themselves. I said I was going to testify, and all the lawyers became visibly upset.

What would I say, they wanted to know. I would say I wasn't there; that I was out of town.

"That sounds like an alibi defense to me, your Honor," one of the government prosecutors said. The Judge, however, couldn't stop me from testifying – it was my right. Nor could he stop me from defending myself.

I took the stand, denied any knowledge of the fire, and said I was out of town that night. I withstood the government prosecutor's cross examination fairly well; it was the old man's lawyer who sunk me.

Before I knew that the old man's was ratting on me, I had written him a letter to remind him of our plan to discredit the State's Attorney, Jim Moore. We had agreed that we would say the Klan had paid Wilson a bribe to protect us in county court if he tried to prosecute us for the tractor thefts. My letter outlined that conversation.

"Have you ever tried to set anybody up", the old man's lawyer asked me. I was angry at even the suggestion.

"No sir," I said.

"Do you recognize this," he asked. He was handing me the letter I had written the old man. I couldn't believe it. Did I write that letter, yes. Was it an attempt to set Jim Moore up on bribery charges – I didn't answer. I was smoking mad. That dirty bastard.

"I don't think you should ask me any more questions," I said. The lawyer realized what I might do – blow the lid off his defense – if he continued, so he stopped. He had gambled that I wouldn't tell on the old man no matter what, and he had won.

"No further questions, Your Honor," he said.

The jury stayed out only a day. It acquitted my mother of the conspiracy charge – she and my dad would later be convicted of the obstruction charges at a separate trial – and convicted the old man and me of all charges.

The press made some comment on the evening news about my shocked appearance upon leaving the courthouse. If they had known what had really happened in that trial, they would have understood why a twenty-two year old boy, going to prison for twelve years, was shocked.

EPILOGE

Fifteen years later I type these words as a reflection on a wasted life. My only hope is that this book will educate you about what the Klan was for me. You can read and tell your children about this and maybe stop one of them from doing what I did. I have taken a great risk in writing this book, as you can imagine. It is worth my life to tell you the truth however. I have been able to live a quiet life since being released, a life without fear of attack from unknown enemies. This book will end that instantly. And although tomorrow is not promised, the message of this book is. That will be enough for me.

Appendix

**THE KLORAN
OF
THE WHITE KNIGHTS
OF
THE KU KLUX KLAN
REALM OF MISSISSIPPI
KLORAN NUMBER_____KLAVERN NUMBER_____
PROVINCE NUMBER_____DISTRICT NUMBER_____
"NON SILBA SED ANTHAR"
HONOR—KHARACTER—DUTY
THE KLAN KREED**

IN THE BEGINNING GOD; ETERNAL, INFINITE CREATOR AND HIS SON, JESUS CHRIST, OUR CRITERION OF CHARACTER, OUR SAVIOUR. IN THIS WE PLACE ALL OUR FAITH.

We know no safe depository of the ultimate powers of society but the people themselves, and if any think them not enlightened enough to exercise their control with wholesome discretion, we believe the remedy is not to take the powers from them, but to inform discretion by education.

We believe there can be no compromise on the matter of the segregation of the Races.

We believe that for any single American citizen to survive the final battle that will be waged by the International Communist Conspiracy, America and its Christian constitutional form of government must survive

We believe with unqualified faith the Holy Bible, **Romans 12:1**, *"we beseech you therefore brethren, by the mercies of God, that ye present your bodies a living sacrifice, Holy, acceptable unto God, which is your reasonable service."*

We believe that the Holy bible and The Constitution of the United States of America are the greatest safeguards of true liberty, justice and the dignity of man ever devised.

We believe that failure to know the enemy, failure to understand him on all fronts, failure to prepare completely t battle him to the ultimate end I defense of this great nation, will give him aid and a comfort. To give the enemy aid and comfort according to the Constitution of the United States of America is treason.

We believe that our future will not redeem our past. We will only drift from one terrible fiasco to another in complete legarthy unless we come to realize that there can be no compromise on the battlefield; no halfway in the fight for the preservation of our religion and freedom; it must be all or nothing. We now rest our case to your courage. Our accusers are persons, not American, our objective if freedom, not peace.

We believe that the crowning glory of a Klansman is to serve-----

NON SILBA SED ANTHAR----------**NOT FOR SELF, BUT FOR OTHERS.**

THE KLAVERN OFFICERS

THE EXALTED CYCLOPS	The president or officer in charge.
THE KALIFF	The vice-president or second officer in charge.
THE KLOKARD OR KLEAGLE	The lecturer, reader and officer who administers the oaths to new members.
THE KLUDD	The Chaplin or religious officer.
THE KLIGRAPH	The secretary.
THE KLABEE	The treasurer.
THE KLADD	The conductor or ceremonial officer.
THE KLAROGO	The inner guard, responsible for the guarding of the inside of the Klavern.
THE KLEXTER	The outer guard, responsible for the guarding of the outside area of the Klavern.
THE KLOKAN	The investigator.
THE KLOKANN	The board of four investigators which are private to the Klokan.
THE KLEPEER	A voting delegate responsible for attending the sessions of the Klanburgesses and representing the Klavern.
THE NIGHT HAWK	The officer in charge of the new men while they await to be inducted.
THE SENATOR	A county officer or voting delegate to sit in the Klonvocation and represent the county there.

THE STANDING KLAVERN COMMITTEES

ALIEN INVESTIGATING COMMITTEE

A committee of an odd number of Klansmen to investigate aliens for their citizenship in the Klan. Only those aliens are investigated who do not receive complete rejection when they are recommended.

MEMBERSHIP COMMITTEE

A committee to insure the regular attendance of all Klansmen and to study those Klansmen who have lax attendance records and make recommendations to the Klavern.

BUILDING COMMITTEE

A committee of three Klansmen to make sure the Klavern has a safe and secret meeting place.

POLITICIAL EDUCTION COMMITTEE

A five man committee to study books, magazines, bookstores, newsstands, newspapers, school books, publications, literature in general, and make the necessary recommendations to the Klavern: To obtain good propaganda and reading material and circulate it among the Klansmen.

VOTER REGISTERATION COMMITTEE

A committee to study the overall and complete voting records in a county: to sponsor voter registration drives of the white people: to study and watch the negro voting activity.

PRINTING COMMITTEE

A committee to secure the secret and proper printing of propaganda for the Klavern.

INTELLIGENCE COMMITTEE

A six man committee of three, two man committees to keep accurate and indexed information on people, places and cars.

SPECIAL COMMITTEES

The Klavern may elect or the Exalted Cyclops may appoint any committees that may be needed to aid the Klavern in accomplishing the purposes of the Klan.

BENEVOLENT COMMITTEE

This committee should send flowers, get well cards, and look after and make reports on sick and needy and Klansmens families in need.

THE KLAVERN ORDER OF BUSINESS

1----Call To Order, Preparation Of Klavern With Holy Bible, Flags and Dedication Fluid.

2----Invocation Prayer By Kludd.

3----Officer Roll Call, Klansmen Roll Call.

4----Klokard And Night Hawk Prepare To Start The Ceremony.

5----Recognition Of Visiting Klansmen And Officers.

6----Recommendation Of Aliens For Citizenship.

7----Reading And Discussion Of Last Meetings Minutes.

8----Klabees Financial Report.

9----Paying Of Dues, Assessments, Etc.

10---Paying Of Bills, Debts, Etc.

11---Old Business, Unfinished Business, Etc.

12---Reading Of Communications, Letters, Etc.

13---Committee Reports, Klansmen In Need, Etc.

14---New And General Business.

15---Induction Ceremony.

16---Announcements Of Klan Ways, Krafts and Projects.

17---Special Committee Reports.

18---Benediction Prayer.

19---Closing Ceremony.

This Order Of Business May Be Altered In A Slight Manner To Suit Any Individual Klavern Circumstances. No Gross Deviation Should Be From This Order Unless Absolutely Necessary.

OPENING CEREMONY

Just prior to the opening of the Klonkleave; the Klaliff will procure the mounted flag and stand it at and in front of his station; The Klokard will procure the altar flag and the unsheathed sword and place same on his station with flag folded compactly; The Kludd will procure the vessel containing the dedication fluid and the Bible and put same on his station; The Night Hawk will procure the Fiery Cross and stand it at and in front of the station of the Exalted Cyclops.

The time having arrived for the opening of the Klonklave, the E. C. (in his absence a substitute) will ascend to his station, and standing will give one rap with his gavel and say:

"ALL PRESENT WHO HAVE NOT ATTAINED CITIZENSHIP IN THE INVISIBLE EMPIRE, KNIGHTS OF THE KU KLUX KLAN, WILL RETIRE TO THE OUTER DEN UNDER THE ESCORT OF THE NIGHT HAWK."

"THE KLEXTER AND THE KLAROGO WILL TAKE THEIR POST AND FAITHFULLY GUARD THE ENTRANCE TO THE KLAVERN."

After all the applicants for membership have been secured, the Klexter and Klarogo will close their respective doors, the Klarogo making his secure. After this is done no one will be allowed to pass the Klarogo into the Klavern until the Klonklave is duly opened. All substitute officers shall be appointed at this time. E. C. will then give three raps with his gavel and take his seat. (The officers do now assume their stations at this time). The E. C. will then command_____

"THE KLADD OF THE KLAN."

The Kladd will advance to a point about five feet in front of the station of the E. C. and say:

"THE KLADD OF THE KLAN YOUR EXCELLENCY!"

E. C.----"You will ascertain with care if all present are Klansmen worthy to sit in the Klavern during the deliberations of this Klonklave."

Kladd----"I HAVE YOUR ODERS, SIR."

The Kladd will then collect from each Klansman present the Countersign and password. As he approaches a Klansman, that Klansman will whisper the words into the ear of the Kladd and resume his seat immediately. If a Klansman should not have the word he will remain standing. The Kladd will proceed around the Klavern to all present. After he had finished he will return to the E. C. and report as follows.

Kladd----"YOUR EXCELLENCY: I RESPECTFULLY REPORT THAT ALL PRESENT ARE KLANSMEN WORTHY OF THE HONOR OF ISTTING DURING THE DELIBERATIONS OF THIS KLONKLAVE." (If any present do not have the words, the Kladd will add to the above): "EXCEPT THOSE STANDING BEFORE YOU; THEY PRESUME TO BE KLANSMEN, BUT THEY DO NOT HAVE THE WORDS."

The E. C. will ask of the Kligrepp if the one standing are worthy; if so, he will instruct them to advance to his station and procure the words. If they are not worthy all ceremony will cease until they become worthy or are ejected from the Klavern. If there be visiting Klansmen present they must be invited to the E. C. station at this time, met by him, then faced toward the sacred altar and introduced to the Klan. All Klansmen will rise and give the TSOG. The visiting Klansmen will return the TSOG. This done the E. C. will give two raps with his gave and say:

"MY TERRORS, YOU WILL TAKE YOUR RESPECTIVE STATIONS AS YOUR NAMES ARE CALLED."

The E. C. sitting in his station will call the roll of officers. When an officers name is called, he will rise and answer: "HERE", and proceed to this station, stand erect and face the Sacred Altar. (If an officer is absent his substitute will rise and say "SUBSTITUTE," and proceed to his station.) When the names of the Klexter and the Night Hawk are called the Klarogo will answer for them if they are present, but if either of them or both of them are absent, the Klarogo will give the names of their substitute and so state.

No one will be allowed to sit on the station of an officer unless by consent of the E. C..

The E. C. will then rise; When he rises the Terrors will face him and salute; he will return the salute and charge them as follows:

"MY TERRORS: YOUR FELLOW KLANSMEN HOLD YOU IN HIGH ESTEEM. YOU HAVE BEEN CHOSEN TO FILL AN IMPORTANT PLACE IN THE AFFAIRS OF THIS KLONKLAVE AND TO SET AN EXAMPLE TO ALL KLANSMEN OF PERFECT OBERSVANCE OF OUR OATH AND DUTIFUL DEVOTION TO UR GREAT FRANTERNITY. THEREFORE, I CHARGE YOU TO DISCHARGE EVERY DUTY INCUMBENT UPON YOU WITH DISPATCH, EFFICIENCY AND DIGNITY,. PRESERVE PEACE AND DECOURM IN OUR DELIBERATIONS AT THIS TIME, AND PRESERVE WITH HONOR IN PROMOTING AND GUARDING WELL AT THIS TIME, AND PRESERVE WITH HONOR IN PROMOTING AND GUARDING WELL EVERY INTEREST OF THE INVISIBLE EMPIRE, KNIGHTS OF THE KU KLUX KLAN".

The E. C. will then give three raps and command:

"MY TERRORS AND KLANSMEN, MAKE READY".

All will rise and put on robes but leave their hood off, and remain standing. (Robing may be omitted if there be no candidates in waiting, at the discretion of the E. C). He will then say:

"PREPARE THE SACRED ALTAR".

The Altar furnishings having been previously placed, the Klokard will advance to the Sacred Altar from his station with the Altar flag and sword; standing on the side of the Sacred Altar next to the Klaliff's station, he will place directly across the center of the Sacred Altar with stars to his left and on opposite edge of flag from him, then turn back upper corner of flag to allow room for vessel of fluid to be placed there without the vessel touching the flag, and then takes position Number 1 facing the Sacred Altar.

As he leaves the Sacred Altar, the Kludd will advance to the Sacred altar with the Holy Bible and vessel of dedication fluid; standing at the point of the sword, he will place the Bible, opened to the 12th Chapter of Romans, on and near the corner of the Sacred Altar to his left and next to him, and the vessel of fluid on and near the corner of sacred Altar to his right and opposite side from him, and takes position Number 2 and faces the Sacred Altar.

As he leaves the Sacred Altar the Night Hawk (in his absence, the Kladd) will advance to the Sacred Altar with the Fiery Cross and place it against center of Sacred Altar on side toward the E. C.'s station, light it, and take position Number 4 facing the Sacred Altar.

The Klokard from his position, carefully surveys the Sacred Altar to make sure it is properly prepared, corrects any imperfections in it preparation, if an; from his position he faces the E. C. (the other three Terrors will do likewise) and address the E. C. as follows:

Klokard----"YOUR EXCELLENCY, THE SACRED ALTAR OF THE KLAN IS PREPARED, THE FIREY CROSS ILLUMINATES THE KLAVERN".

E. C.----"FAITHFUL KLOKARD, WHY THE FIREY CROSS?"

Klokard----"SIRE, IT IS THE EMBLEM OF THAT SINCERE, UNSELFISH DEVOTEDNESS OF ALL KLANSMEN TO THE SACRED PURPOSE AND PRINCIPLES WE HAVE NOW ESPOUSED."

E. C.----"MY TERRORS AND KLANSMEN, WHAT MEANS THE FIREY CROSS?"

All----"WE SERVE AND SACRIFICE FOR THE RIGHT."

E. C.----"KLANSMEN ALL: YOU WILL GATHER FOR OUR OPENING DEVOTIONS."

When he says this he will rise and advance to and occupy the position Number 2 occupied by the Kludd; as he approaches the Kludd that Terror will advance to the Sacred Altar and take position near the point of the sword.

All Klansmen will form on the quadrate, forming straight lines between these four positions; these four positions occupied by Terrors, form the corners of the quadrate. The Terrors, in taking these positions should step out far enough to accommodate the members between them, about an equal number on each side of the quadrate. The distance between the Klansmen in this quadrate should be about three feet. If there be more than enough to form one line and so on until all are in position. Great care must be exercised to form the quadrate correctly and symmetrically with the Sacred Altar in as near the exact center as possible. When the formation is complete all will join in the singing of the following Klode:

My Country, 'Tis Of Thee, Sweet Land Of Liberty, Of Three I Sing, Land Where My Fathers Died, Land Of The Pilgrims Pride, From Every Mountain Side, Let Freedom Ring.

Our Fathers God! To Three, Author Of Liberty, To Thee We Sing, Long May Our Land Be Bright, With Freedoms Holy Light, Protect Us By Thy Might, Great God Our King!

After singing, the Kludd at the Sacred Altar leads in the following prayer. (All must stand with bowed Heads).

"OH GOD OUR HEAVENLY GUIDE, AS FINITE CREATURES OF TIME AND AS DEPENDENT CREATURES OF THINE, WE ACKNOWLEDGE THE AS OUR SOVERIGN LORD. PERMIT FREEDOM AND THE JOYS THEREOF TO FOREVER REIGN THROUGHOUT OUR LAND. MY WE AS KLANSMEN FOREVER HAVE THE COURAGE OF OUR CONVICTIONS AND THAT WE MAY ALWAYS STAND FOR THEE AND OUR GREAT NATION. MAY THE SWEET CUP OF BROTHERLY FRATERNITY EVER BE OURS TO ENJOY AND BUILD WITHIN US THAT WISDOM KINDRED TO HONORABLE DECISIONS AND THE GODLY WORK. BY THE POWER OF THY INFINITE SPIRIT AND THY ENERGIZIG VIRTURE THEREIN. EVER KEEP BEFORE US OUR OATHS OF SECRECY AND PLEDGES OF RIGHTEOUSNESS. BLESS US NOW I THIS ASSEMBLY THAT WE MAY HONOR THEE IN ALL THINGS, WE PRAY IN THE NAME OF CHRIST, OUR BLESSED SAVIOUR." "AMEN." "All Klansmen say Amen."

After the prayer all, facing the Sacred Altar, will give together TSOG and holding same will say, "FOR MY COUNTRY, THE KLAN, MY FELLOW KLANSMEN AND MY HOME." Then all will give the N. H. to the flag. The E. C. then immediately returns to his station; as he vacates position Number 2, the Kludd will advance from the Sacred Altar and occupy the position Number 2. As the E. C. steps into station, faces the assembly, and gives one rap with his gavel, at this each Klansman will face him and give TSOTF-C, then TSOC-1, then raise TSOS, and then TSOK-G; as he responds with TSOK-C they will recover. He holds TSOK-C and says:

"MY TERRORS AND KLANSMEN; IN THE SACRED CAUSE WE HAVE ENTERED, BE THOU FAITHFUL UNTO DEATH; BE PATRIOTIC TOWARD OUR COUNTRY; BE KLANISH TOWARD KLANSMEN; BE DEVOTED TO OUR GREAT FRATERNITY."

He then recovers TSOK-C, and says: "MY TERRORS AND KLANSMEN: WHAT IS THE SWORN DUTY OF A KLANSMAN IN KLONKLAVE ASSEMBLED?"

All answer together----"TO MAINTAIN PEACE AND HARMONY IN ALL THE DELIBERATIONS OF THE KLAN IN KLONKLAVE ASSEMBLED, AND TAKE HEED TO INSTRUCTIONS GIVEN."

The E. C. will then give two raps with his gavel. All will be seated and he will say:

"I NOW OFFICIALLY PROCLAIM THAT HIS KLONKLAVE OF _____ KLAVERN NUMBER_____REALM OF MISSISSIPPI OF THE INVISIBLE EMPIRE, KNIGHTS OF THE KU KLUX KLAN, DULY OPENED FOR THE DISPATCH OF BUSINESS."

"FAITHFUL KLAROGO: YOU MAY NOW ADMIT ALL QUALIFIED KLANSMEN, BUT GUARD WELL THE PORTAL TO THIS KLAVERN. THE NIGH HAWK (in his absence the Kladd) WILL EXTINGUISH THE FIREY CROSS."

He gives one rap with his gavel and takes his seat and proceeds with the regular order of business.

****

CLOSING CEREMONY

The order of business having been finished, the E. C. will rise and give one rap with is gavel and say:

"MY TERRORS AND KLANSMEN; THE SACRED PURPOSE OF THE GATHERING OF THE KLAN AT THIS TIME HAS BEEN FULFILLED; THE DELIBERATIONS OF THIS KLONKLAVE HAVE ENDED."

E. C.----"FAITHFUL KLALIFF: WHAT IS THE FOURFOLD DUTY OF A KLANSMAN?"

The Klaliff will rise and say:

"TO WORSHIP GOD: BE PATRIOTIC TOWARD OUR COUNTY: BE DEVOTED AND LOYAL TO OUR KLAN AND ITS OFFICES AND TO PRACTICE KLANISHNESS TOWARD HIS FELLOW KLANSMEN." (remains standing).

E. C.----"FAITHFUL KLUDD: HOW SPEAKETH THE ORACLES OF OUR GOD?"

The Kludd will rise and say:

"THOU SHALT WORSHIP THE LORD THY GOD. RENDER UNTO THE STATE THE THINGS WHICH WARE THE STATE'S. LOVE THEY BROTHERHOOD: HONOR THE KING. BEAR YE ONE ANOTHERS BURDENS, AND SO FULFILL THE LAW OF CHRIST." (and the Kludd remains standing).

E. C.----"FAITHFULL KLOKARD: WHAT DOES A KLANSMAN VALUE MORE THAN LIFE?'

The Klokard will rise and say:

"HONOR TO A KLANSMAN IS MORE THAN LIFE." (and remains standing).

E. C.----"FAITHFULL KLADD: HOW IS A KLANSMAN TO PRESERVE HIS HONOR?"

The Kladd will rise and say:

"BY THE DISCHARGE OF DUTY IN THE FAITHFUL KEEPING OF HIS OATH." (and remains standing).

E. C.----"WHAT SAY YOU MY TERRORS?"

All the other officers will rise and say together:

"YOUR EXCELLENCY: THE IMMACULATE TRUTH HAS BEEN SPOKEN.": (and remain standing).

E. C.----"WHAT SAY YOU MY FELLOW KLANSMEN?"

All members will rise and say together: "AMEN" (and remain standing).

E. C.----"MY TERRORS AND KLANSMEN: YOU KNOW WELL THE DUTY OF A KLANSMAN; BE THOU NOT RECREANT TO DUTYS DEMAND AS WE GO HENCE FROM THIS KLAVEN TO ENTER THE STRESSFUL STRUGGLE OF THE ALIEN WORLD. PROTECT YOUR HONOR BY KEEPING INVOILATE YOUR SACRED OATH."

The E. C. then gives one rap with his gavel, and give the SOK-C which is answered by all. All will recover the SOK-C together.

E. C.----"THE CROWNING GLORY OF A KLANSMAN IS TO SERVE, "NON SILBA SED ANTHAR." (All will say: "Not for self, but for others.") "LET US BE FAITHFUL IN SERVING OUR GOD, OUR COUNTRY, OUR EMPEROR AND OUR FELLOW KLANSMN."

The E. C. will then give on rap with his gavel and say:

"MY FAITHFUL KLANSMEN: AS PEACE DWELLS AMONG US YOU WILL ASSEMBLE FOR OUR PARTING DEVOTIONS.

All will assemble in the quadrate formed as in the opening ceremony (the Klarogo and Klexter making secure their respective doors), the Kludd stands at the Sacred Altar. All will stand facing the Sacred Altar and come to the SOTF-C hands resting palms on back of each, thus paralleling the ARS, and will join in singing the following Klode. (tune-Bless Be The Tie That Binds).

"BLEST BE THE KLANSMANS TIE, OF REAL FRATERNAL LOVE, THAT BINDS US IN A REAL FELLOWSHIP, AKIN TO THAT ABOVE."

Each will then stand with left hand over the heart and the right resting on the left shoulder of the Klansman to the right.

E. C.----"KLANSMEN: UNITED IN THE SACRED BOND OF KLANISH FIDELITY WE STAND, BUT DIVIDED BY SELFISHNESS AND STRIFE WE FALL: SHALL WE STAND OR SHALL WE FALL?"

All will answer:

"WE WILL STAND: FOR OUR BLOOD IS NOT SHED IN VAIN."

Each Klansman will then join in singing the following Kloxology: (Tune-America)

"GOD OF ETERNITY, GUARD, GUIDE OUR GREAT COUNTRY, OUR HOMES AND STORE, KEEP OUR GREAT STATE TO THEE, IT'S PEOPLE RIGHT ANDFREE, IN US THEY GLORY BE, FOREVERMORE."

After the singing all will look to the mounted flag and will give GTNH and then stand with bowed heads; The Kludd standing at the Sacred Altar will pronounce the Benediction:

"OUR HEAVENLY FATHER WE INVOKE THY DIVINE BENEDICTION UPON US. KEEP US UNFETTERED FROM THE WORLD THAT WE MIGHT FIGHT THE GOOD FIGHT, RUN A TRUE COURSE AND E WORTHY TO CLAIM THE PRIZE. MAY WE AS BRETHERN AND KLANSMEN BE STEADFAST AND UNREMOVABLE, ALWAYS ABOUNDING IN THE WORK OF OUR LORD KNOWING THAT OUR LABOR IS NOT IN VAIN. THROUGH JESUS CHRIST WE PRAY, AMEN. (All will say, "AMEN").

The benediction having been said, the E. c. will immediately return to his station, give one rap with his gavel and say:

"I NOW OFFICIALLY PROCLAIM THAT THIS KLONKLAVE OF_____ KLAVERN NUMBER_____ REALM OF MISSISSIPPI OF THE INVISIABLE EMPIRE, THE WHITE KNIGHTS OF THE KU KLUX KLAN, DULY CLOSED, WE WILL GATHER AGAIN ON _____. He will then say:

'KLANSMAN ONE AND ALL" SAYING this he will LTOS and all will do likewise. All will then give and hold TSOG, and the E. C. will say:

"TO YOU, FAITHFUL KLANSMEN, GOOD NIGHT."

Then all will say: "YOUR EXCELLENCY, GOOD NIGHT." He and they will recover TSOG together, The E. C. gives one rap and announces:

"THE KLADD AND NIGHT HAWK WILL GATHER AND MAKE SECURE THE PROPERTIES OF THE KLAN."

"THE KLAN IS DISMISSED, FAITHFUL KLAROGO: YOU WILL OPEN THE PORTAL SO THAT ALL KLANSMEN MAY PASS TO THE OUTER WORLD.

Before going out each Klansman will see that the robe worn by him is securely cared for and well hidden if same is to be carried home by him.

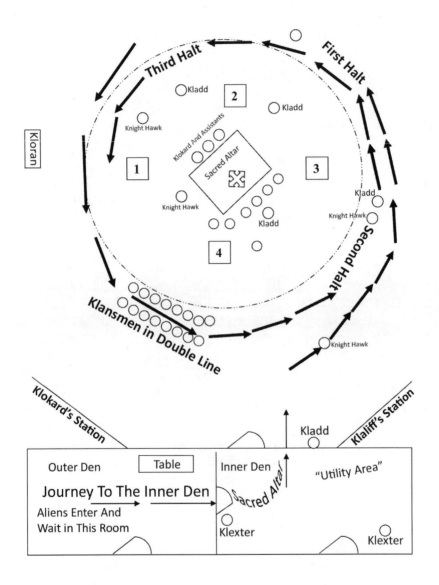

NATURALIZATION CEREMONY
OF
THE WHITE KNIGHTS OF THE KU KLUX KLAN
REALM OF MISSISSIPPI

When the ceremony of naturalization shall have been reached in the regular order of business, the Klarogo will signal by ALLW to the Klexter, who will repeat the signal to the Night Hawk in the Outer Den with the candidates. Prior to the signal to the Night Hawk in the Outer Den with the candidates, Prior to the signal the Night Hawk will have presented a blank petition for citizenship to each candidate, requesting him to read and sign same. (Said petition to be witnessed by the Night Hawk). He will collect from each candidate the Kloctoken, if same has not been previously paid. On hearing the signal the Kloxter will approach the outer door of the Inner Den and give three on seven (7) raps (having in his possession the petitions and Klectokens of the waiting candidates).

KLEXTER----"WHO DARES APPROACH SO NEAR THE ENTRANCE TO THIS KLAVERN."

NIGHT HAWK----"THE NIGHT HAWK OF THE KLAN."

KLEXTER----"ADVANCE WITH THE COUNTERSIGN." (The Night Hawk then will whisper the countersign through the door).

KLEXTER----"PASS."

The Night Hawk will pass into the Inner den and enrobe completely. Then he will approach the door to the Inner Klavern and give three raps. When the Klarogo opens the door the Night Hawk will GALLW.

KLAROGO----"WHO SEEKS ENTRANCE TO THE INNTER KLAVERN."

NIGHT HAWK----"THE NIGHT HAWK OF THE KLAN WITH IMPORTANT INFORMATION AND DOCUMENTS FROM THE ALIEN WORLD FOR HIS EXCELLENCY."

The Klarogo reports and salutes to the E. C.

KLAROGO----"YOUR EXCELLENCY: THE NIGHT HAWK OF THE KLAN IS RESPECTFULLY WITING TO ENTER THE KLAVERN WITH IMPORTANT INFORMATION AND DOCUMENTS FROM THE ALIEN WORLD."

E.C.----"YOU WILL PERMIT HIM TO ENTER."

The Klarogo returns to the door and gives ALLW and is answered by the Night Hawk with a LLW, then the Klarogo opens the door and say:

"YOU HAVE PERMISSION OF HIS EXCELLENCY TO ENTER."

The night Hawk enters, stands erect and GTSOG; All will answer the same from their seats. The Night will then proceed t the Sacred Altar. He will GTNH, then GTSOFC, then removes his hood and GTSOK-C, and stands erect and ready.

E. C.----"FAITHFUL NIGHT HAWK, YOU MAY NOW SPEAK AND IMPART THE IMPORTANT INFORMATION IN YOUR POSSESSION TO US."

NIGHT HAWK----(Bowing First) "YOUR EXCELLENCY: SIR, PURSUAT TO MY DUTY IN SEEKING LAUDABLE ADVENTURE IN THE ALIEN WORLD, I FOUND THESE MEN. (here he gives their names). THEY HAVING READ THE IMPERIAL PROCLAMATION OF OUR EMPEROR, AND PROMPTED BY UNSELFISH MOTIVES, DESIRE A MORE NOBLE LIFE. IN CONSEQUENCE THEY HAVE MADE THE HONORABLE DECISION TO FORSAKE THE WORLD OF SELFISHNESS AND FRATERNAL ALIENATION AND EMIGRATE TO THE DELECTABLE BOUNDS OF THE INVISABLE EMPIRE AND BECOME LOYAL CITIZENS OF SAME."

E.C.----"FAITHFUL NIGHT HAWK: THIS IS INDEED IMPORTANT INFORMATION, MOST PLEASANT TO HEAR. IMPRTANT IN THAT IT EVIDENCES HUMAN PROGRESS: MOST PLEASANT IN THAT IT REVEALS THROUGH YOU A KLANSMANS SINCERE APPRECIATION OF HIS SACRED MISSION AMONG MEN AND HIS FIDELITY TO DUTY IN THE BETTERMENT OF MANKIND, THEIR RESPECTIE PETITIONS WILL BE RECEIVED AND JUSTLY CONSIDERED."

NIGHT HAWK----(Bowing First) "SIR, I HAVE IN MY POSSESSION THE REQUIRED PETITIONS FOR CITIZENSHIP OF THE MEN NAMED, TOGETHER WITH THEIR KLECTOKEN."

E. C.----"YOU WILL DELIVER THEM TO THE KLIGRAPH WHO WILL READ THEM TO ALL KLANSMEN ASSEMBLED."

The Night Hawk will deliver the petitions to the Kligraph along with the Klectokens and resume his position at the Altar. The Kligraph will then rise and read the names and give the petitions to the E. C. and resume his sea.

E. C.----"KLANSMEN, YOU HAVE HEARD THE NAMES OF PETITIONERS FOR CITIZENSHIP IN THE INVISIABLE EMPIRE. DOES ANY KLANSMAN O HIS OATH OF ALLEGIANCE, KNOW ANY JUST REASON WHY THESE ALIENS, OR ANY OF THEM, SHOULD BE DENIED CITIZENSHIP IN THE INVISABLE EMIRE."

If there be no objections the E. C. will address the Night Hawk:

E. C.----"FAITHFUL NIGHT HAWK, YOU WILL INFORM THESE ALIEN PETITIONERS FROM ME."

"THAT IT IS THE CONSTANT DISPOSITION OF A KLANSMAN TO ASSIST THOSE WHO ASPIRE TO THINGS NOBLE IN THOUGHT AND CONDUCT, AND TO EXTEND A HELPING HAND TO THE WORTHY. THAT THEIR DESIRES ARE SINCERELY RESPECTED, THEIR M,ANLY PETITIONS ARE BEING SERIOUSLY CONSIDRED IN THE LIGHT OF JUSTICE AND HONOR. WITH TRUE FAITH A MAN MAY EXPECT A JUST OF JUSTICE AND HONOR. WITH TRUE FAITH A MAN MAY EXPECT A JUST ANSWER TO HIS PRAYERS AND HIS VIRTUOUS HOPES WILL ULTIMATELY RIPEN INTO A SUBLIME FRUTATION."

The Night Hawk bows and says: "I HAVE YOUR ORDERS SIR." then retires to the outer door of the inner den of the Klavern and through the wicket of the outer door informs the candidates as follows.

"WORTHY ALIENS, HIS EXCELLENCY THE EXALTED CYCLOPS, BRING THE DIRECT REPRESENTATIVE OF HIS MAJESTY, OUR EMPEROR, AND CHIEF GUARDIAND OF THE PORTAL OF THE INVISIBLE EMPIRE, HAS OFFICIALLY INFORMED ME TO INFORM YOU THAT IT IS THE CONSTANT DISPOSITION OF A KLASMAN TO ASSIST THOSE WHO ASPIRE TO THINGS NOBLE IN THOUGHT AND CONDUCT AND TO EXTEND A HELPIG HAND TO THE WORTHY. THEREFORE YOUR DESIRES ARE SINCERELY RESPECTED AND YOUR MANLY PETITIONS ARE BEING SERIOUSLY CONSIDERED IN THE LIGHT OF JUSTICE AND HONOR. WITH TRUE FAITH OU MAY EXPECT A JUST ANSWER TO YOUR PRAYERS, AND YOUR VIRTUOUS HOPES MAY EXPECT A JUST ANSWER TO YOUR PRAYERS, AND YOUR VIRTUOUS HOPES WILL ULTIMATELY RIPEN INTO A SUBLIME FRUTATION, THIS IS THE DECISION OF HIS EXCELLENCY, THE EXALTED CYCLOPS, WITH ALL HIS KLAN CONCURRING."

The Night Hawk then returns to his station in the Klavern without form.

E. C. ----"FAITHFUL KLOKARD: YOU WILL EXAMINE UNDER WITNESS THE ALIEN PETITIONES AS TO THEIR QUALIFICATIONS."

The Klokard with his assistants, the Klaliff and Kludd, retires to the outer den and will propound to the candidates in waiting the following required "Qualifying Interrogatories."

Klokard----'EACH OF THE FOLLOWING QUESTIONS MUST BE ANSWERED BY A LOUD AND EMPATHIC YES."

1----IS THE MOTIVE PROMPTING YOUR AMBITION TO BE A KLANSMAN SERIOUS AND USLEFISH? _____

2----ARE YOU A NATIVE BORN WHITE, GENTILE AMERICAN CITIZEN? _____

3----ARE YOU ABSOLUTELY FREE OF AND OPPOSED TO ANY ALLEGIANCE OF ANY NATURE TO ANY CAUSE, GOVERNMENT, PEOPLE, SECT OR RULER THAT IS FOREIGN TO THE UNITED STATES OF AMERICA? _____

4----DO YOU BELIEVE IN THE TENENTS OF THE CHRISTIAN RELIGION? _____

5----DO YOU ESTEEM THE UNITED STATES OF AMERICA AND ITS INSTITUTIONS ABOVE ANY OTHER GOVERNMENT, CIVIL, POLITICAL, ECCLESIASTICAL IN THE WHOLE WORLD? _____

6----WILL YOU, WITHOUT MENTAL RESERVATION, TAKE A SOLEM OATH TO DEFEND, PRESERVE AND PROTECT SAME? _____

7----DO YOU BELIEVE IN KLANISHNESS AND WILL YOU PRACTICE SAME FAITHFULLY TOWARDS KLANMEN? _____

8----DO YOU BELIEVE IN AND WILL YOU FAITHFULLY STRIVE FOR THE ETERNAL MAINTENANCE OF WHITE SUPREMACY? _____

9----WILL YOU FAITHFULLY OBEY OUR CONSTITUION AND LAWS, AND CONFORM WILLINGLY TO ALL OUR USAGES, REQUIREMENTS AND REGULATIONS? _____

10---CAN YOU ALWAYS BE DEPENDED ON? _____

This done, he, with his assistants, will return to the Sacred Altar, he will salute and report as follows:

"YOUR EXCELLENCY, THESE _____ MEN IN WAITING HAVE EACH DULY QUALIFIED TO ENTER OUR KLAVERN TO JOURNEY THROUG THE MYSTIC CAVE IN QUEST OF CITIZENSHIP IN THE INVISIBLE EMPIRE."

E. C.----"THE KLADD OF THE KLAN!" The Kladd will rise and advance to a position about five feet from the E. C. and say:

"THE KLADD, YOUR EXCELLENCY."

E. C.----"YOU WIL RETIRE UNDER SPECIAL ORDERS TO THE OUTER PREMISES OF THE KLAVERN, ASSUME CHARGE OF THE WORTHY ALIENS IN WAITING, AND AFFORD THEM A SAFE JOURNEY FROM THE WORLD OF SELFISHNESS AND FRATERNAL ALIENTATION TO THE SACRED ALTAR OF THE EMPIRE OF CHIVALARY, INDUSTRY, HONOR AD LOVE."

The Kladd salutes the E. C. and says: "I HAVE YOUR ORDERS SIR!"

He then retires to the room where the candidates are, lines the up in single file, the left hand of the rear man on the left shoulder of the man in front of him. He then takes his place in front of them and says: "FOLLOW ME." "BE A MAN (OR MEN)." He then proceeds to the outer door of the inner den and gives thereon *0.

KLEXTER----(opening the wicket and saying) "WHO AND WHAT IS YOUR BUSINESS."

KLADD----"I AM THE KLADD OF THIS KLAN ACTING UNDER SPECIAL ORDERS OF HIS EXCELLENCY, OUR EXALTED CYCLOPS; I AM IN CHARGE OF A PARTY!"

KLEXTER----"WHAT E THE NATURE OF YOUR PARTY."

KLADD----"WORTHY ALIENS FROM THE WORLD OF SELFISHNESS AND FRATERNAL ALIENTATION, PROMPTED BY UNSELFISH MOTIVE, DESIRE THE HONOR OF CITIZENSHIP IN THE INVISIABLE EMPIRE AND THE FELLOWSHIP OF KLANSMEN."

KLEXTER----"HAS YOUR PARTY BEEN SELECTED WITH CARE?"

KLADD----"THESE ARE KNOWN AND HAVE BEEN VOUCHED FOR BY KLANSMEN IN KLONKLAVE ASSEMBLED."

KLEXTER----"HAVE THEY HAD THE MARKS?"

KLADD----"THE DISTINGUISHING MARKS OF A KLANSMAN ARE NOT FOUND IN THE FIBRE OF HIS GARMENTS OR HIS SOCIAL OR FINANCIAL STANDING. THEY ARE SPIRITUAL: NAMELY A CHIVALRIC HEAD, A COMPASSIONATE HEART, A PRUDENT TOUGNE AND A COURAGEOUS HEART. ALL DEVOTED TO OUR COUNTRY, OUR KLAN, OUR HOMES AND EACH OTHER: THESE ARE THE DISTINGUISHING MARKS OF A KLANSMAN, OH FAITHFUL KLEXTER: AND THESE CLAIM THE MARKS."

KLEXTER----"WHAT IF ONE OF YOUR PARTY SHOULD PROVE HIMSELF TO BE A TRAITOR?"

KLADD----"HE WOULD BE IMMEDIATELY BANISHED IN DISGRACE FROM THE INVISIBLE EMPIRE WITHOUT FEAR OR FAVOR, CONSCIENCE WOULD BE TENACIOUSLY TORMENT HIM, REMORSE WOULD REPEATEDLY REVILE HI M, AND DIREFUL THINGS WOULD BEFALL HIM."

KLEXTER----"DO THEY KNOW ALL THIS?"

KLADD----"ALL THIS THEY NOW KNOW, HAVE HEARD AND MUST HEAD."

KLEXTER----"FAITHFUL KLADD, YOU SPEAK THE TRUTH."

KLADD----"FAITHFUL KLEXTER, A KLANSMAN SPEAKETH THE TRUTH IN AND FROM HIS HEART. A LYING SCOUNDREL MAY WRAP HIS DISGRACEFUL FRAME WITHIN THE FOLDS OF A KLANSMANS ROBE AND DECIEVE THE VERY ELECT BUT ONLY A KLANSMAN POSSESESS A KLANSMANS HEART AND A KLANSMANS SOULD."

KLEXTER----"ADVANCE WITH THE COUNTERSIGN."

Then only the Kladd advances and through the wicket whispers the countersign to the Klexter.

KLEXTER----(opening the wicket) "WITH HEART AND SOUL I TE KLEXTER OF THIS KLAN WELCOME YOU AND OPEN THE WAY FOR YOU TO ATTAIN THE MOST NOBLE ACHIEVEMENT IN YOUR EARTHLY CAREER. BE FAITHFUL AND TRUE UNTO DEATH AND ALL WILL BE WELL AND YOUR REWARD SURE. NOBLE KLADD YOU WILL PASS WITH YOUR PARTY.

The Kladd with his part will pass the outer door and stop. He will then give ALLW, and the Klarogo upon hearing the LLW will then announce:

"YOUR EXCELLENCY AND KLANSMEN ASSEMBLE: I HEAR THE SIGNAL OF THE KLADD OF THE KLAN ON HIS WAY WITH A PARTY."

E. C.----"MY TERRORS AND KLANSMEN, ONE AND ALL: MAKE READY!"

Each Klansman will put on his hood both aprons down, all robes completely buttoned. All lights must be turned down so as to make the Klavern almost dark. All must remain still and quiet. Only the officers who must read will use a light and then only a small light. When all are ready, the Klarogo will answer the Kladd with ALLW, and begin to OTDS.

KLADD----"SIRS, THE PORTAL TO THE INVISIBLE EMPIRE IS BEING OPENED FOR YOU. YOUR RIGHTEOUS PRAYER IS BEING ANSWERED FOR YOU AND YOU HAVE FOUND FAVOR IN THE SIGHT OF THE EXALTED CYCLOPS AND HIS KLANSMEN ASSEMBLED. FOLLOW ME AND BE PRUDENT."

As the Kladd approaches the inner door with his party, the Klarogo will stop them by facing them with TSOF-C. he will then recover TSOF-C, face inward and stand erect and ready. (The Klokard or his assistant before this has stationed himself just inside the door and not seen by the party but to be heard by them) will say:

"God give us men! The Invisible Empire demands strong,

Minds, great hearts, true faith and ready hands,

Men whom the lust of office does not kill,

Men whom the lust of office cannot buy,

Men who posses an opinion and a will,
Men who have Honor, and men who will not Lie,
Men who can stand before a demagogue,
And dam his treacherous flatteries without winking,
Tall men, sun crowned, who live above the fog,
In public duty and private thinking,
For while the rabble, with their thumb worn creeds,
Their large professions and little deeds,
Mingle in selfish strife, Lo! Freedom weeps,
Men who serve not for selfish booty,
But real men, courageous, who flinch not at duty,
Men of dependable character, Men of sterling worth,
Then wrongs will be redressed, and right will rule the earth,
GOD GIVE US MEN!!!!

KLAROGO----"WILL EACH OF YOU AS KLANSMEN IN YOUR DAILY LIFE ALWAYS ERNESTLY ENDEAVOR TO BE AN ANSWER TO THIS PRAYER?" _____ He then faces the E. C. and says?

"YOUR EXCELLENCY AND FELLOW KLANSMEN: JUST SUCH MEN ARE STANDING IN THE PORTAL OF THE INVISIBLE EMPIRE, DESIRING THE LOFTY HONOR OF CITIZENSHIP THEREIN, READY AND WILLING TO FACE VERY DUTY ON HIM THAT MAY BE IMPOSED.

E. C.----:FAITHFUL KLAROGO AND KLANSMEN, LET THEM ENTER THE KLAVERN IN QUEST OF CITIZENSHIP, BUT YOU KEEP A KLANSMANS EYE UPON THEM, AND IF ANY ONE OF THEM SHOULD FLINCH, SHOW UP AS A COWARD, OR AS A SCALAWAG NOW OR AT ANY TIME IN THE FUTURE, IT WILL BE YOUR DUTY TO THEN EJECT HIM OR THEM FROM THE PORTAL OF THE INVISIBLE EMPIRE AND DO SO WITHOUT DELAY: BE HTOU NOT RECREANT TO DUTYS DEMANDS."

While the above prayer is being said the Night Hawk takes the fiery cross from the Altar, lights it and takes position in front of and abut four feet from the Klaliffs station, facing the Klarogo, holding the fiery cross above his head.

The Klarogo steps aside and will say to the Kladd, "PASS."

When the Kladd crosses the threshold of the Klavern he will stop ad give TSOG. All Klansmen except the officers, will rise, face the Kladd, and give TSOG, face the altar and remain standing with TSOC-L. The Kladd will then proceed with his party toward the Night Hawk. As the Kladd will then proceed with his party toward the Night Hawk. As the Kladd approaches the Night Hawk and gets abut six feet from him the Night Hawk will about face and march in front of him on the journey until his is halted by ALLW from the E. C. When he hears the signal he will stop his party, answer the signal with ALLW, then face his party toward the Sacred Altar. When this is done the Night Hawk with the fiery cross takes a position in front of and about six feet from the party, facing the party with the cross uplifted. He will remain here until he hears the second LLW from the E. C. Then he will resume his position in front of the Kladd and move n with the party. When the Kladd hears the same LLW he will face his party as they were, answer the LLW with ALLW and follow the Night Hawk.

When the signal of ALLW of the E. C. is first given, all Klansmen except the station officers, Klarogo and Klexter will form from the seats, march around the hall in single file, the Klokard leading to his right, pass in front along the line of the party, between the party and the Night Hawk, with each Klansmen looking the party right in the eyes but moving on, and after passing the party the Klokard will form the Klansmen in a double line with open ranks about six feet apart and facing each other, holding TSOC-L, and standing steady on the opposite side of the Klavern; The E. C. then gives the second LLW and the Night Hawk will lead the Kladd and his party on their journey by way of the E. C. station and through the formation of the Klansmen. All this must be done with quiet and dignity.

After the Kladd and his part have passed the formation of the Klansmen, all Klansmen will without signal return to their seats but will remain standing until the Kladd presents his party to the E. C. and then they will quietly sit down.

As the Kladd approaches the station of the Klaliff after he has passed the formation of the Klansmen, the Klaliff will rise and GTSOG and halt him with ALLW. On hearing it the Kladd and Night Hawk stops and the Kladd answers with same.

Klaliff----"WHO ARE YOU THAT WALK IN THE KLAVERN AT THIS HOUR?"

KLADD----"FAITHFUL KLALIFF, THESE ARE MEN LIKE THE INVISIBLE EMPIRE AND THE TIMES DEMAND: MEN OF STRONG MINDS AND GREAT HEARTS: TRUE AND FAITHFUL WITH READY HANDS: WORTHY ALIENS KNOWN AND VOUCHED FOR AND ON ORDERS OF HIS EXCELLENCY, I, THE KLADD OF THE KLAN, AM THEIR GUIDE OT THE SACRED ALTAR."

KLALIFF----"PASS."

The journey from the entrance to the E. C. station must be made in a circle around the Klavern.

The Night Hawk will move on, followed by the Kladd and his party and will continue until he arrives at the station of the E. C. where he shall stop and line his company up in a straight line in front of the station. The Night Hawk stops but does not change his position. The Kladd steps to the rear of the party and will say:

"YOUR EXCELLENCY, ON YOUR ORDERS I PRESENT YOU THESE MEN OF REAL DEPENDABLE CHARACTER AND COURAGE, WHO ASPIRE TO THE LIFE AND NOBLE HONOR OF CITIZENSHIP IN THE INVISILE EMPIRE."

The E. C. will rise and address the candidates as follows:

"SIRS? IS THE MOTIVE PROMPTING YOUR PRESENCE HERE SERIOUS AND UNSELFISH?" _____

"IT IS INDEED REFRESHING TO MEET FACE TO FACE WITH MEN, WHO BY ACTING ON MANLY MOTIVES, ASPIRE TO ALL THINGS NOBLE FOR YOURSELVES AND HUMANITY."

"THE LUSTRE OF THE HOLY LIGHT OF CHIVALRY HAS LOST ITS FORMER GLORY AND IS SADL DIMMED BY THE CHOKING DUST OF SELFISH SORDID GAIN. PASS ON."

The E. C. will resume his seat, and the Kladd will face his party toward the Night Hawk and advance behind the Night Hawk until he hears the signal of ALLW from the Klokard. On hearing the signal from the Klokard, the Night Hawk stops and stands steady, the Kladd will also stop his party immediately in front of the Klokard's station and fame them to the Klokards station and answer the signal by the same. On hearing the answer the Klokard will rise, address the party as follows:

"REAL FRATERNITY, BY SHAMEFUL NEGLECT, HAS BEEN STARVED UNTIL SO WEAK HER VOICE IS LOST IN THE COURTS OF HER OWN CASTLE, AND SHE PASSES UNNOTICED BY HER SWORN SUBJECTS AS SHE MOVES ALONG THE REAL MAN IS BY THE STANDARD OF WEALTH AND NOT WORTH: SELFISHNESS IS REAL AND EVERY RELIGIOUS CONVICTION TO DO HOMAGE TO HER AND YET WITH THE CRUEL HEART OF JEZEBEL SHE SLAUGHTERS THE SOULS OF THOUSANDS OF HER DEVOTEES DAILY. PASS ON."

The Klokard will resume his seat, and the Kladd will face his party as before, advancing behind the Night Hawk until he hears the signal of ALLW from the Klaliff. On hearing the signal the Night Hawk stops and stands steady; the Kladd will stop his party in front of the Kladd's stations, facing them to the Klaliff and then giving ALLW. Then the Klaliff will rise and say:

"THE UNSATISFIED THIRST FOR GAIN IN DETHRONING REASON AND THE JUDGMENT IN THE CITADEL OF THE HUMAN SOUL, AND MAN MADDENED THERBY FORGETS HIS

PATRIOTICE, DOMESTIC AND SOCIAL OBLIGATIONS AND DUTIES AND FENDISHELY FIGHTS FOR A PLACE IN THE FAVOR OF THE GODDESS OF GLITTERING GOLD: THEY STARVE THEIR OWN SOULS: THEY MAKE SPORT OF SPIRITUAL DEVELOPMENT. PASS ON."

The Klaliff will resume his seat, and the Kladd will face his party as before and advance behind the Night Hawk until he hears the ALLW from the Kludd. On hearing this the Night Hawk stops and stands steady; the Kladd will also stop his party in front of the Kludd's station, facing them to the Kludd, then giving ALLW. Upon hearing this, the Kludd will rise and address the party as follows:

"MEN SPEAK OF LOVE AND LIVE IN HATE,
MEN TALK OF FAITH AND TRUST FATE,
OH, MIGHT MEN DO THE THINGS THEY TEACH,
OH, MIGHT MEN LIVE THE LIFE THEY PREACH,
THEN THE THRONE OF AVARICE WOULD FALL,
AND THE CLANGOR OF GRIM SELFISHNESS,
OVER THE EARTH WOULD CEASE,
LOVE WOULD TREAD OUT THE BALEFUL FIRE OF ANGER,
AND IN ITS ASHES PLANT THE LILY OF PEACE, PASS ON."

The Kladd will resume his seat and the Kladd will face his party as before, advancing behind the Night Hawk until he hears the signal of the E. C. who will give ALLW. Then the Night Hawk stops and goes to take position at the Sacred Altar. The Kladd will stop his party in front of the E. C. station and face them toward it. He will then give ALLW. Then the E. C. will rise and say:

"SIRS, WE CONGRATULATE YOU ON YOUR MANLY DECISION TO FORSAKE THE WORLD OF SELFISH AND FRATERNAL ALIENATION AND IMIGRATE TO THE BOUNDS OF THE INVISIBLE EMPIRE AND BECOME LOYAL CITIZENS OF THE SAME. THE PRIME PURPOSE OF THIS GREAT ORDER IS TO DEVELOP CHARACTER, PRACTICE KLANISHENESS, TO PROTECT THE HOME OF YOURS, THE CHASITY OF THE WOMANHOOD, AND TO EXEMPLIFY A PURE PATRIOTISM TOWARDS OUR GREAT COUNTY."

YOU, AS CITIZENS OF THE EMPIRE, MUST BE ACTIVELY PATRIOTIC TOWARDS OUR COUNTRY AND CONSTANTLY KLANISH TOWARDS KLANSMEN, SOCIALL, PHYSICALLY, MORALLY, AND VOCATIONALLY; WILL YOU ASSUME THIS BINDING OBLIGATION OF CITIZENSHIP." _____

"YOU MUST UNFLINCHINGLY COFORM TO OUR USAGES, REQUIREMENTS, REGULATIONS AND WORDS IN EVERY DETAIL, AND PROVE YOURSELVES WORTHY TO HAVE AND TO HOLD THE HONORS WE BESTOW: DO YOU FREELY AND FAITHFULLY ASSUME TO DO THIS?" _____

"IF YOU HAVE ANY DOUBT AS TO YOUR ABILITY TO QUALIFY, EITHER IN BOD OR CHARACTER, AS CITIZENS OF THE INVISIBLE EMPIRE, YOU NOW HAVE AN OPPORTUNITY TO RETIRE FROM THIS PLACE WITH THE GOOD WILL OF THE KLAN. I WARN YOU NOW, IF YOU FALTAR OR FAIL NOW OR IN THE FUTURE, IN KLONKLAVE OR IN LIFE, YOU WILL BE BANISHED FROM CITIZENSHIP IN THE INVISIBLE EMPIRE WITHOUT FEAR OR FAVOR."

THIS IS A SERIOUS UNDERTAKING: WE ARE NOT HERE TO MAKE SPORT OF YOU NO INDULGE IN THE SILLY FRIVOLITY OF CIRCUS CLOWNS. BE YOU WELL ASSURED HE THAT PUTTETH HIS HAND TO THE PLOW AND LOOKETH BACK IS NOT FIT FOR THE KINDGOM OF HEAVING; OR WORTHY OF HIGH HONOR OF CITIZENSHP IN THE INVISIBLE EMPIRE. DO NOT DECEIVE YOURSELVES, YOU CANNOT DECEIVE US AND WE WILL NOT BE MOCKED. DO ANY OF YOU WISH TO LEAVE?" _____

"FAITHFUL KLOKARD, YOU WILL DIRECT THE WAY FOR THESE ALIENS TO THE SACRED ALTAR OF THE EMPIRE OF CHIVALRY, HONOR, INDUSTRY AND LOVE, IN ORDER THAT THEY MIGHT MAKE FURTHER PROGRESS TOWARD ATTAINING THE CITIZENSHIP IN THE INVISIBLE EMPIRE, THE WHITE KNIGHTS OF THE KU KLUX KLAN, REAL OF MISSISSIPP."

The Kladd will conduct the party to the Sacred Altar by way of the Klokard's station. When he has arrived within about six fee of the Klokard's station, he will turn square to his left and continue in a

Straight direction until he reaches a point of about six feet of the Sacred Altar toward the station of the E. C. He will then turn square to his right and continue until he has passed the Sacred Altar about four feet; he will then turn square to his left and continue until he passes the Sacred Altar about six feet; then he will turn square to his left and bring his party into a sort of hollow square around the Sacred Altar. If he has few candidates he may form a straight line facing them to the Sacred Altar on the Klaliff side, looking to the E. C. stations and finish forming the hollow square with Klansmen.

The Night Hawk will take his place with the Fiery Cross held a lot just from the corner of the Sacred Altar to the right of the E. C. He will stand within the quadrate. The Fiery Cross is held a lot in and during the administering of the oaths and the dedicatory ceremony.

The first paragraph above gives a general idea regarding the real journey of the candidates to the Sacred Altar as to turns, angles and distances. In the ceremony as in the journey, the size of the group and the good judgment of the Kladd will get the best results in forming the ceremonial acts.

The Kladd should study his part well. The floor work is very, very important and impressive. He should exercise good mannerisms and a military style in is work.

When the Klokard has perfect the quadrate around the Altar, he will advance to a point midway between the Sacred Altar and the station of the E. C., salute and clearly say:

"YOUR EXCELLENCY, THE ALIENS IN OUR MIDST FROM THE WORLD OF THE SELFISH AND FRATERNAL ALIENATION, FORSAKE THE PAST AND ARE NOW READY AND WILLING TO BIND THEMSELVES BY AN UNYIELDING THE TO THE INVISIBLE EMPIRE, THE WHITE KNIGHTS OF THE KU KLUX KLAN OF MISSISSIPPI."

Then the Kladd will about face and advance to his position opposite of the center and to the rear of the line of candidates towards the station of the Klaliff, and await orders.

The Klokard with his assistants, the Klaliff and the Kludd will, with steady pace, form across the open side of the hollow square, so as to evenly complete the square, this being done the Klokard or his assistants will then administer the Oath.

****

THE OATH

The candidates will raise their right hand and place their left hand over their heart and say "I" then pronounce their full name.

I _____CONSCIOUSLY, WILLINGLY AND SOBERLY STANDING IN THE PRESENCE OF ALMIGHTY GOD _____ AND THESE MYSERTIOUS KLANSMEN _____ DO HEREBY PLEDGE, SWEAR AND DEDICATE MY MIND, MY HEART, AND MY BODY _____ TO THE HOLY CAUSE OF PRESERVING CHRISTIAN CIVILIZATION THE DIGNITY AND INTERGITY OF THE HOLY WRIT____AND THE CONSTITUTION OF THE UNITED STATES OF AMERICA AS ORIGINALLY WRITTEN____AS THE GREATEST SAFEGUARDS OF JUSTICE AND TRUE LIBERTY EVER WRITTEN____I SWEAR THAT I WILL

PRESERVE, PROTECT AND DEFEND____THE CONSTITUTION OF THE WHITE KNIGHTS OF THE KU KLUX KLAN OF MISSISSIPPI____ AND OEY THE LAWS ENACTED THEREUNDER____AND THE LAWFUL ORDERS OF THE OFFICERS OF THE KLAN.

I SWEAR THAT I WILL WHOLEHEARTEDLY, EMBRACE____ THE SPIRIT OF CHRISTIAN MILITANCY____WHICH IS THE BASIC PHILOSOPHY OF THIS ORDER. I SWEAR THAT I WILL PRAY FOR DAILY GUIADANCE____TO HELP ME DETERMINE MY PROPER BALANCE____BETWEEN THE HUMBLE AND THE MILITANT APPROACH TO MY PROBLEMS, IN ORDER THAT MY ARMS SHALL ALWAYS REMAIN____AS INSTRUMENTS OF JUSTICE____IN THE HANDS OF ALMIGHTY GOD____AND NOT BECOME TOOLS OF MY OWN VENGANCE____I SWEAR THAT I WILL CONSTANTLY PREPARE MYSELF____PHYSICALLY, MORALLY, MENTALLY AND SPIRITUALLY____IN ORDER THAT I MAY BECOME AN INCREASINGLY USEFUL INSTRUMENT____IN THE HANDS OF ALMIGHTY GOD____AND THAT HIS WILL BE DONE THRU ME____AS PART OF HIS DIVINE PURPOSE. I SWEAR THAT I WILL REMAIN CONSTANTLY ALERT____TO THE SATANIC FORCE OF EVIL____WHICH IS, AND SHALL REMAIN____MY ETERNAL ENEMY. I SWEAR THAT I WILL OPPOSE AND EXPOSE THIS FORCE____AT EVERY OPPORTUNITY____IN MY KLONKLAVE AND IN LIFE. I SWEAR THAT I WILL OFFER THE UTMOST OF BOTH____MY PHUSICAL COURAGE____AND MY MORAL COURAGE____WHICH MAY REQUIRE THE SACRIFICE____OF MU EGO AND PRESTIGE IN DAILY LIFE. I HEREBY DEDICATE MY BEING____NOT ONLY TO COMBAT SATAN____BUT GOD WILLING____TO THE TRIUMPH____OVER HIS MALIGNANT FORCES____AND AGENTS HERE ON EARTH. NOT ONLY WILL I DIE____IN ORDER TO PRESERVE CHRISTIAN CIVILIZATION____ BUT I WILL LIVE AND LABOR MIGHTLY____TO LIVE FOR THE SPIRIT OF CHRIST IN ALL MEN, I SWEAR THAT I WILL CLEAVE TO MY BRETHEN____IN THIS ORDER AND THEIR FAMILIES____ ABOVE_____

ALL OTHERS____AND WILL DEFEND AND PROTECT THEM____AGAINST ALL OF OUR ENEMIES____BOTH DOMESTIC AND FOREIGN. I SWEAR THAT I WILL NEVER____BE THE CAUSE OF A BREACH F SECRECY____OR ANY OTHER ACT____THAT MAY BE DETRIMENTAL____TO THE INTEGRITY OF____THE WHITE KNIGHTS OF THE KU KLUX KLAN OF MISSISSIPPI. ALL OF THESE THINGS____I DO SWEAR TO DO____AND I WILL DAILY

BESEECH GOD____MY CREATOR AND SAVIOUR____THAT I MAY
BE GRANTED____THE STRENGTH____THE ABILITY____AND
THE GRACE____THAT I MAY BE EMINENTLY SUCCESSFUL____
IN MY PERFORMANCE____OF THIS SACRED OBLIGATION. I
DO HEREBY BIND MYSELF____TO THIS OATH____UNTO MY
GRAVE____SO HELP ME ALMIGHTY GOD.

After the Oath, the Klokard will about face and advance to a point about halfway between the Altar and E. C.'s station. He will salute and say:

" YOUR EXCELLENCY, THE WORTHY ASPIRANTS AT THE SACRED LTAR OF THE KLAN HAVE EACH VOLUNTARILY ASSUMED, WITHOUT MENTAL RESERVATION, THE SOLEM AND THRICE BINDING OATH OF THE KLAN AND ARE WAITING TO BE DEDICATED TO THE HOLY SERVICE OF OUR COUNTRY, THE KLAN, EACH OTHER, OUR HOMES, AND HUMANITY."

E. C.----"FAITHFUL KLOKARD, YOU AND YOUR ASSISTANTS HAVE PERFORMED YOUR DUTY WELL AND NOW YOU MAY REST. STAND READY SHOULD SOME OTHER DUTY ARISE."

The Klokard resumes his place in the quadrate formation between his assistants. The E. C. will then proceed to the Sacred Altar to perform the following dedication ceremony.

****

DEDICATION

E. C.----"SIRS, HAVE EACH OF YOU ASSUMED WITHOUT MENTAL RESERVATION YOUR OATH F ALLEGIANCE TO THE INVISIBLE EMPIRE?" _____

"MORTAL MAN CANNOT ASSUME A MORE BIND OATH: CHARACTER AND A COURAGE ALONE WILL ENABLE YOU TO KEEP IT. ALWAYS REMEMBER THAT TO KEEP IT MEANS TO YOU HONOR, HAPPINESS AND LIFE: BUT, TO VIOLATE IT MEANS DEATH, DISHONOR AND DISGRACE. MAY HONOR, HAPPINESS AND LIFE BE YOURS."

Then the E. C. holds up the vessel containing the dedication fluid and addresses the candidates as follows:

"WITH THIS TRANSPARENT LIFE GIVING, POWERFUL GOD GIVEN FLUID, MORE PRECIOUS AND FAR MORE SIGNIFICANT THAN ALL THE SACRED OILS OF THE ANCIENTS, I SET YOU APART FROM THE MEN OF YOUR DAILY ASSOCIATION TO THE GREAT AND HONORABLE TASK YOU HAVE VOLUNTARILY ALLOTED TO

YOURSDELVES AS CITIZENS OF THE INVISIBLE EMPIRE, THE WHITE KNIGHTS OF THE KU KLUX KLAN, RELM OF MISSISSIPPI. AS A KLANSMAN MAY YOUR CHARACTER ALWAYS E AS TRANSPARENT, YOUR LIFE PURPOSE AS POWERFUL, YOUR MOTIVE IN ALL THINGS AS MAGNANIMOUS AND AS PURE, AND YOUR KLANISHNESS AS REAL AND AS FAITHFUL AS THE MANIFOLD DROPS HEREIN, AND YOU A VITAL BEING AS USEFUL TO HUMANITY AS IS WATER TO MANKIND. YOU WILL NOW KNEEL ON YOUR RIGHT KNEE."

Just here the following stanza must be sung in a soft but distant tone, preferably by a quartet.

Tune****Just as I am without one plea.

To The, Oh God I Call To The,

True To My Oath Oh Help Me Be,

I've Pledged My Love, M Blood, My All,

H, Give Me Grace That I May Not Fall.

****

E. C.----"SIRS, NEATH THE UPLIFTED FIERY CROSS WHICH BY ITS HOLY LIGHT LOOKS DOWN UPON YOU TO BLESS WITH ITS SACRED TRADITIONS OF THE PAST."

"I DEDICATE YOU IN BODY, IN MIND, IN SPIRIT AND IN LIFE, TO THE HLY SERVICE OF OUR COUNTY, OUR KLAN OUR HOMES, EACH OTHER AND HUANITY."

He then goes to the candidates and puts a few drops on each others back and say, "IN BODY", then puts a few drops on his head and says "IN MIND, then with a few drops on his hands, tosses it upwards and says "IN SPIRIT", then moves his hand in a circular motion around the candidates head and will say "AND IN LIFE."

"THUS DEDICATED BY US, NOW CONSECRATE YOURSELVES TO THE SACRED CAUSE YOU HAVE ENTERED."

"MY TERRORS AND KLANSMEN, LET US PRAY."

THE DEDICATORY PRAYER

All except those officiating at the Altar must kneel, with the E. C. stepping back to the rear and left of the Kludd; the Night Hawk remains still; the Kludd will move close to the Sacred Altar on the side of the E. C.'s station and will offer the following prayer.

"OUR HEAVENLY FATHER, WE BESEECH THEE THAT AN OVERWHELMING SENSE OF DEDICATION WILL EMBRACE THESE MEN KNEELING BEFORE THEE. LOOK ON THAT TO WHICH THEY ASPIRE WITH FAVOR AND BLESS THEM IN THAT WHICH THEY HOPE TO OVERCOME. DEDICATE THEM, THEREFORE, TO THE FIGHT FOR RIGHT, FREEDOM, AND A KLANMAN LIKE SPIRIT. ALLOW THE NOBLE ATTITUDES OF HONOR, TRUTH, AND BROTHERLY AFFILIATION TO EVER PERMEATE THEIR LIVES THEIR HONOR, THEIR HOMES AND IDEALS. THROUGH CHRIST OU LORD WE PRAY. AMEN. (All will then say AMEN).

After the prayer all will rise, the E. C. will step to the Altar and instruct the candidates to rise. The Kludd will step back to his place and the E. C. will then address the candidates as follows:

"YOU ARE NO LONGER STRANGERS OR ALIENS AMONG US, BUT ARE CITIZENS WITH US; AND WITH CONFIDENCE THAT YOU HAVE NOT SWORN FALSELY OR WITH DECIET IN YOUR OATH. I, ON BEHALF OF OUR EMPEROR AND ALL KLANSMEN NOW WELCOME YOU TO CITIZENSHIP IN THE EMPIRE OF CHIVALRY, HONOR, INDUSTRY AND LOVE."

Then the E. C. will raise the front of his hood and all Klansmen will do likewise as a token of welcome and he will greet each of the candidates with TCOK, then returns to his position and says:

"BY AUTHORITY VESTED IN ME BY OUR EMPORERO, I NOW DECLARE AND PROCLAIM YOU AS CITIZENS OF THE INVISIBLE EMPIRE, THE WHITE KNIGTS OF THE KU KLUX KLAN, REALM OF MISSISSIPPI, THE MOST HONORABLE AMONG MEN, A KLANSMAN."

This done, the E. C. returns to his station and the candidate is greeted under the Fiery Cross by each Klansman, by TCOK. This being done, the E. C. will say:

"THE KLADD OF THE KLAN."

KLADD----"THE KLADD YOUR EXCELLENCY."

E. C.----"YOU WILL ESCORT THESE KLANSMEN AT THE ALTAR TO THE KLOKARD WHO WILL SEE THAT THEY GET THE SIGNS, WAYS, WORDS, GRPS, AND WAYS OF THE KLAVERN."

KLADD----"I HAVE YOUR ORDERS."

The Klockard may give the instructions himself or appoint a party to retire to the Outer Den to instruct the new Klansmen.

THE WAY OF THE KLAVERN

The ways of the Klavern are never written but are passed person to person. Below is listed the overall way to securely operate the Klavern.

1----The Password is set by the Klexter and Klarogo on their duly appointed substitutes. It is changed frequently. The Klexter will give the password when the Klansmen are arriving and he has ascertained that all are safe to let pass after having recognized them by the signs, ways, words and grips. The Klarogo will then collect the password from the arriving Klansmen as they enter the Klavern.

2----The duly authorized officers of the Klan will instruct the duly elected officers of the Klavern as to ways, words, signs and grips.

3----No one is allowed in the Klavern unless he is able to give the necessary signs, ways, words and grips to the Klexter or in some cases be vouched for by a Klansmen so recognized.

4----If the signs, ways, words and grips are ever changed the Klan will be so instructed by the responsible officers.

THE KLONVERSATION

The Invisible Empire	The Ku Klux Klan
A Realm	The Ku Klux Klan Of A State
District	A Territory Within A State
Province	A Territory Within A District
Klanton	A Territory Within A Province Or The Jurisdiction Of A Klavern
Klavern	A Unit Of The Klan Within A Province
Klonklave	The Klavern Or The Klan Gathered In Secret Session.
Klanburgesses	The Lower House of The Klongress
Klonvocation	The Upper House Of The Klongress
Klongress	The Legislature Of The Klan
Klabursar	A District Treasurer Of The Klan
Klanjustice	A District Judge Within The Realm
Province Investigator	An Investigative Province Officer
Province Giant	An Administrative Province Officer
Province Titan	A Military Province Officer
Province Fury	A Military Province Officer
Kleagle	An Organizer For The Klan
Klan Kleagle	The Realm Officer In Charge Of The Klan Organization
Grand Director Of The Klan Bureau Of Investigation	The Realm Investigative Officer
Grand Chaplin	The Realm Religious Office
Grand Giant	The Realm Administrative Officer
Grand Dragon	A Realm Executive Officer, Second Highest Authority In The Realm

Imperial Wizard	The Highest Executive Authority Of The Realm
Anno Klan	In The Year Of The Klan, Thus Ak
The Kloran	The Book Of The Klan, This Book
Imperial Order	The Order Of The Imperial Wizard
Grand Order	The Order Of A Grand Office
Lawful Order	The Lawful Order Of Any Officer Or The Klan

IMPERIAL ORDERS

This Kloran is to always be guarded with the utmost of security and never used unless in complete secrecy or in Klonklave. It is to e stored when not in use in a safe place where no person r alien will ever lays eyes on it.

This Kloran is to always be considered the property of the White Knights of the Ku Klux Klan of Mississippi and should such occasion arise that it is necessary to cease using this Kloran, any proper demand by any such grand officer shall compel Klansmen to surrender same.

Extreme care should always be taken in the handling and use of the Kloran to insure its lasting. It should never be folded, bent, wet or soiled in any manner. It is numbered and all Klaverns which shall receive copies shall be held accountable.

The Grand Giants Office shall be the issuing and responsible grand officer for the Klorans in every detail. This Kloan is so manufactured as pages can be taken from or added to in the future, but, no alteration whatsoever will ever be made unless on the lawful orders of the Grand Giant.

The Imperial Authority Of The
White Knights Of The Ku Klux Klan
Realm Of Mississippi
April 20, 98 AK

Manufactured By: RR Donnelley
                     Breinigsville, PA USA
                     October, 2010